WordPress Respo Theme Design

Develop and customize your very own responsive
WordPress themes quickly and efficiently

Dejan Markovic

[PACKT] open source*
PUBLISHING   community experience distilled

BIRMINGHAM - MUMBAI

WordPress Responsive Theme Design

First published: June 2015

Production reference: 1260615

Published by Packt Publishing Ltd.
Livery Place
35 Livery Street
Birmingham B3 2PB, UK.

ISBN 978-1-78528-845-6

www.packtpub.com

Credits

Author
Dejan Markovic

Reviewers
Rory Ashford
John Eckman
Mattia Migliorini

Commissioning Editor
Dipika Gaonkar

Acquisition Editors
Neha Nagwekar
Larissa Pinto

Content Development Editor
Rohit Kumar Singh

Technical Editors
Mrunal M. Chavan
Rahul C. Shah

Copy Editors
Sonia Michelle Cheema
Gladson Monteiro
Vikrant Phadke
Stuti Srivastava
Neha Vyas

Project Coordinator
Mary Alex

Proofreaders
Simran Bhogal
Safis Editing
Maria Gould

Indexer
Monica Ajmera Mehta

Production Coordinator
Nilesh R. Mohite

Cover Work
Nilesh R. Mohite

About the Author

Dejan Markovic is the president of NYTO Group (http://www.nytogroup.com/), a premium web development company with offices conveniently located in both Toronto and New York. He is an experienced web developer with the extensive knowledge of both frontend and backend technologies (PHP, ASP.NET, JavaScript, ColdFusion, HTML5, CSS3, WordPress, Joomla, Drupal, to name just a few).

As Dejan strongly believes in returning back to the community, he developed and contributed to 2 free WordPress plugins: Buffer My Post (https://wordpress.org/plugins/buffer-my-post/) and Tweet Old Custom Post (https://wordpress.org/plugins/tweet-old-custom-post/). He is also one of the organizers of WPToronto meetup group and the WordCamp Toronto, an annual WordPress conference.

You can always find him on various WordCamps (especially the ones within driving distance from Toronto) or exploring the nature, art & love for food across Canada & US. Should you have any questions, comments, concerns or just want to say hello, you can shoot him an email at dejan@dejanmarkovic.com. He would love to hear your thoughts about this book.

Dejan was a technical reviewer of the book *Learning Yeoman* (http://www.amazon.com/Learning-Yeoman-Jonathan-Spratley/dp/1783981385). This is his first time as an author.

I would like to thank my girlfriend, life partner, and future wife, Tina, who always stood beside me through my best and worst times. Thank you for your help and understanding, and your tremendous and unconditional support. Without you, all of this would have been impossible. Tina, you are my shining star!

I would also like to thank my mother, Spasenija, who is still my inspiration and a great example of a survivor who went through a lot. Thank you Mama for everything!

This book would not have been possible without the support and love of my brother, Marko, my beautiful sister-in-law, Nikolina, and the best nephews and niece anyone could have—Stefan, Luka, and Angelina. I love you all very much and thank you for your understanding (especially my nephews and niece) as I had to work on this book even while staying at your home during the holidays. I am so sorry that I didn't have more free time to play with you.

My soon-to-be brother-in-law, Tosha Serbian, has created the logo for the theme Topcat that we used in this book. Tosha, thank you for your help and advice. It is greatly appreciated!

Many thanks to Neha Nagwekar, Neetu Mathew, Rohit Kumar Singh, Larissa Pinto, and the rest of the Packt Publishing team.

I have recently lost two family members that were important to me, and this section is dedicated to them:

Our beloved Dragisa,

You've left us quietly, as you have lived your entire life. Your heart, which taught us honesty, integrity, and loyalty, has stopped. We are left here alone, without you, with all those memories of true appreciation and friendship. Your time was colored with modesty, generosity, and self-sacrificing and strenuous work. You were our backbone in the hardest times and with your generosity you accepted us as your own. We will be forever grateful. May you have eternal glory!

Dear Noki,

You were the light that was shining on us. Your passion to help everybody and your reliability are something that people will remember you by.

I will never forget you and I will always love you with all my heart. Your will be my brother forever!

About the Reviewers

Rory Ashford is an English web developer. He currently manages the studio at Code Blue Digital. In his spare time, he has built the Gridtacular responsive grid system, Wordpress BEM Menus, and other open source projects.

> I would like to thank my girlfriend, Caroline, for her patience (and her coffee). She put up with me when reviewing this book in the midst of buying and moving into our new house.

John Eckman is the chief executive officer of 10up, a distributed digital agency that focuses on designing and delivering great web publishing experiences on WordPress.

He received a BA from Boston University, a master's degree in information systems from Northeastern University, and a PhD from the University of Washington, Seattle. John is an active contributor to a number of open source projects and communities, and a founder and organizer of WordCamp Boston. He posts blogs at `www.openparenthesis.org` and tweets as `@jeckman`.

Mattia Migliorini, also known as deshack, is a freelance web designer and developer who loves WordPress. He is always on the lookout for amazing responsive designs. He is also an open source evangelist and a member of the Ubuntu community. Mattia currently works both as a freelancer and for VB Italia Srl, an Italian e-commerce company.

www.PacktPub.com

Support files, eBooks, discount offers, and more

For support files and downloads related to your book, please visit www.PacktPub.com.

Did you know that Packt offers eBook versions of every book published, with PDF and ePub files available? You can upgrade to the eBook version at www.PacktPub.com and as a print book customer, you are entitled to a discount on the eBook copy. Get in touch with us at service@packtpub.com for more details.

At www.PacktPub.com, you can also read a collection of free technical articles, sign up for a range of free newsletters and receive exclusive discounts and offers on Packt books and eBooks.

https://www2.packtpub.com/books/subscription/packtlib

Do you need instant solutions to your IT questions? PacktLib is Packt's online digital book library. Here, you can search, access, and read Packt's entire library of books.

Why subscribe?

- Fully searchable across every book published by Packt
- Copy and paste, print, and bookmark content
- On demand and accessible via a web browser

Free access for Packt account holders

If you have an account with Packt at www.PacktPub.com, you can use this to access PacktLib today and view 9 entirely free books. Simply use your login credentials for immediate access.

Table of Contents

Preface

If you want to leave your mark in the wonderful world of WordPress, then continue reading. This book will teach you how to develop and customize your very own responsive theme in WordPress. The added benefits for you are that you will get a lot of useful tips and tricks throughout the book intended to make your life easier. We will provide you with the essentials in the development of the responsive theme in WordPress and the rest is up to you and your imagination!

What this book covers

Chapter 1, Responsive Web Design with WordPress, introduces you to the concepts and techniques of responsive web design and walks you through the process of setting up a WordPress environment.

Chapter 2, Understanding the WordPress Theme Structure, teaches you about the WordPress theme architecture and the purpose of the most important template files.

Chapter 3, Getting Started with Responsive Layout, starts your development journey where you will learn how to choose the right tool for your project (text editor or IDE), how to set up functions.php and styles.css, set fonts and font-icons, add morenizr.js and respond.js essential scripts, and how to add media queries.

Chapter 4, Learn How to Create the Header and Navigation, teaches you about the most important component of any website—navigation!

Chapter 5, Customizing Single Post Templates, focuses on the post templates and their components: title, meta, and navigation. In this chapter, we are setting up a basic layout that we will later expand with the index templates and static pages.

Chapter 6, Responsive Widgets, Footer, and Comments, introduces you to the magic world of widgets, footer, sidebar, and comments with a lot of useful tips and tricks.

Chapter 7, Working with Images and Videos, starts with something fun and, as some might say, the most interesting components of any website—images and videos. In this chapter, you will learn about featured images, image captions, image galleries, and how to work with videos.

Chapter 8, Working with Template Files, focuses on the most important files for the WordPress themes. In this chapter, you will understand the WordPress template hierarchy, understand the functionality of archive pages and you will find excerpts on how to customize the paging navigation, style and sticky post, and also how to modify archive.php, 404.php, and search.php.

Chapter 9, Working with Static Pages and Adding the Extra Functionality with Plugins, wraps up the development part of our book. In this chapter, you will learn about static pages, sliders, shortcodes, how to make your home page responsive, and how to make the contact us page.

Chapter 10, Submitting Your Theme to WordPress.org, covers how to test your theme and polish your code before the submission, and helps you learn how to submit your theme to the WordPress.org repository.

What you need for this book

The software applications that are recommended for this project are XAMPP, WAMP, and MAMP please choose one that fits your needs. Also, it would be beneficial to have the WordPress installed locally or on the hosted environment.

Who this book is for

This book is intended for all of you WordPress enthusiasts who want to develop and customize your very own WordPress responsive theme. Some knowledge of WordPress, PHP, MySQL, HTML, and CSS is expected from you.

Conventions

In this book, you will find a number of text styles that distinguish between different kinds of information. Here are some examples of these styles and an explanation of their meaning.

Code words in text, database table names, folder names, filenames, file extensions, pathnames, dummy URLs, user input, and Twitter handles are shown as follows: "Make sure that the theme directory is named `topcat` and not `topcat_start`."

A block of code is set as follows:

```
@media only screen and (max-width: 480px) {
  //mobile styles
  // up to 480px size
}
```

When we wish to draw your attention to a particular part of a code block, the relevant lines or items are set in bold:

```
<div id="page" class="hfeed site topcat_page">
```

New terms and **important words** are shown in bold. Words that you see on the screen, for example, in menus or dialog boxes, appear in the text like this: "The tagline can be found and set in `wp-admin` by navigating to **Settings | General**."

> Warnings or important notes appear in a box like this.

> Tips and tricks appear like this.

Reader feedback

Feedback from our readers is always welcome. Let us know what you think about this book—what you liked or disliked. Reader feedback is important for us as it helps us develop titles that you will really get the most out of.

To send us general feedback, simply e-mail feedback@packtpub.com, and mention the book's title in the subject of your message.

If there is a topic that you have expertise in and you are interested in either writing or contributing to a book, see our author guide at www.packtpub.com/authors.

Customer support

Now that you are the proud owner of a Packt book, we have a number of things to help you to get the most from your purchase.

Downloading the example code

You can download the example code files from your account at http://www. packtpub.com for all the Packt Publishing books you have purchased. If you purchased this book elsewhere, you can visit http://www.packtpub.com/support and register to have the files e-mailed directly to you.

Downloading the color images of this book

We also provide you with a PDF file that has color images of the screenshots/ diagrams used in this book. The color images will help you better understand the changes in the output. You can download this file from http://www.packtpub.com/ sites/default/files/downloads/8456OS_ColorImages.pdf.

Errata

Although we have taken every care to ensure the accuracy of our content, mistakes do happen. If you find a mistake in one of our books—maybe a mistake in the text or the code—we would be grateful if you could report this to us. By doing so, you can save other readers from frustration and help us improve subsequent versions of this book. If you find any errata, please report them by visiting http://www.packtpub. com/submit-errata, selecting your book, clicking on the **Errata Submission Form** link, and entering the details of your errata. Once your errata are verified, your submission will be accepted and the errata will be uploaded to our website or added to any list of existing errata under the Errata section of that title.

To view the previously submitted errata, go to https://www.packtpub.com/books/ content/support and enter the name of the book in the search field. The required information will appear under the **Errata** section.

Piracy

Piracy of copyrighted material on the Internet is an ongoing problem across all media. At Packt, we take the protection of our copyright and licenses very seriously. If you come across any illegal copies of our works in any form on the Internet, please provide us with the location address or website name immediately so that we can pursue a remedy.

Please contact us at copyright@packtpub.com with a link to the suspected pirated material.

We appreciate your help in protecting our authors and our ability to bring you valuable content.

Questions

If you have a problem with any aspect of this book, you can contact us at questions@packtpub.com, and we will do our best to address the problem.

1
Responsive Web Design with WordPress

Responsive web design (RWD) is a web design approach aimed at crafting sites to provide an optimal viewing experience – easy reading and navigation with a minimum of resizing, panning, and scrolling – across a wide range of devices (from mobile phones to desktop computer monitors).

Reference: http://en.wikipedia.org/wiki/Responsive_web_design.

To say it simply, **responsive web design (RWD)** means that the responsive website should adapt to the screen size of the device it is being viewed on.

When I began my web development journey in 2002, we didn't have to consider as many factors as we do today.

We just had to create the website for a 17-inch screen (which was the standard at that time), and that was it. Yes, we also had to consider 15, 19, and 21-inch monitors, but since the 17-inch screen was the standard, that was the target screen size for us. In pixels, these sizes were usually 800 or 1024. We also had to consider a fewer number of browsers (Internet Explorer, Netscape, and Opera) and the styling for the print, and that was it.

Since then, a lot of things have changed, and today, in 2015, for a website design, we have to consider multiple factors, such as:

- A lot of different web browsers (Internet Explorer , Firefox, Opera, Chrome, and Safari)
- A number of different operating systems (Windows (XP, 7, and 8), Mac OS X, Linux, Unix, iOS, Android, and Windows phones)
- Device screen sizes (desktop, mobile, and tablet)

- Is content accessible and readable with screen readers?
- How the content will look like when it's printed

 Throughout the book, we will use the RWD abbreviation for responsive web design, the IE abbreviation for Internet Explorer, and the FF abbreviation for Firefox browsers.

Today, creating different design for all these listed factors and devices would take years. This is where a responsive web design comes to the rescue.

In this chapter, we will cover:

- The concepts of RWD
- Techniques in RWD
- Setting up the WordPress environment

The concepts of RWD

I have to point out that the mobile environment is becoming more important factor than the desktop environment. Mobile browsing is becoming bigger than the desktop-based access, which makes the mobile environment very important factor to consider when developing a website. Simply put, the main point of RWD is that the layout changes based on the size and capabilities of the device its being viewed on. The concepts of RWD, that we will learn next, are: Viewport, scaling and screen density.

Controlling Viewport

On the desktop, Viewport is the screen size of the window in a browser. For example, when we resize the browser window, we are actually changing the Viewport size.

On mobile devices, the Viewport size is also independent of the device screen size. For example, Viewport is 850 px for mobile Opera and 980 px for mobile Safari, and the screen size for iPhone is 320 px.

If we compare the Viewport size of 980 px and the screen size of an iPhone of 320px, we can see that Viewport is bigger than the screen size. This is because mobile browsers function differently. They first load the page into Viewport, and then they resize it to the device's screen size. This is why we are able to see the whole page on the mobile device.

If the mobile browsers had Viewport the same as the screen size (320 px), we would be able to see only a part of the page on the mobile device.

In the following screenshot, we can see the table with the list of Viewport sizes for some iPhone models:

				Search: iphone	
Device Name ⬍	Platform ⬍	Pixel Density ⬍	Screen Size ⬍	Portrait Viewport Width ⬍	Landscape Viewport Width ⬍
Apple iPhone 3G	iOS	163dpi	3.5"	320	480
Apple iPhone 3GS	iOS	163dpi	3.5"	320	480
Apple iPhone 4	iOS	326dpi	3.5"	320	480
Apple iPhone 4S	iOS	326dpi	3.5"	320	480
Apple iPhone 5	iOS	326dpi	4"	320	568

We can control Viewport with CSS:

```
@viewport {width: device-width;}
```

Or, we can control it with the `meta` tag:

```
<meta name="viewport" content="width=device-width">
```

In the preceding code, we are matching the Viewport width with the device width.

Because the Viewport `meta` tag approach is more widely adopted, as it was first used on iOS and the `@viewport` approach was not supported by some browsers in this book, we will use the `meta` tag approach.

We are setting the Viewport width in order to match our web content with our mobile content, as we want to make sure that our web content looks good on a mobile device as well.

> We can set Viewports in the code for each device separately, for example, 320 px for the iPhone. The better approach will be to use `content="width=device-width"`.

Scaling

Scaling is extremely important, as the initial scale controls the zoom aspect of the content for the initial look of the page. For example, if the initial scale is set to 3, the content will be loaded in the size of 3 times of the Viewport size, which means 3 times zoom. Here is the look of the screenshot for initial scale=1 and initial scale=3:

As we can see from the preceding screenshots, on the initial scale 3 (three times zoom), the logo image takes the bigger part of the screen.

It is important to note that this is just the initial scale, which means that the user can zoom in and zoom out later, if they want to.

Here is the example of the code with the initial scale:

```
<meta name="viewport" content="width=device-width, initial-scale=1, maximum-scale=1">
```

In this example, we have used the `maximum-scale=1` option, which means that the user will not be able to use the zoom here. We should avoid using the `maximum-scale` property because of accessibility issues. If we forbid zooming on our pages, users with visual problems will not be able to see the content properly.

The screen density

As the screen technology is going forward every year or even faster than that, we have to consider the screen density aspect as well. Screen density is the number of pixels that are contained within a screen area. This means that if the screen density is higher, we can have more details, in this case, pixels in the same area.

There are two measurements that are usually used for this, **dots per inch** (**DPI**) and **pixels per inch** (**PPI**). DPI means how many drops a printer can place in an inch of a space. PPI is the number of pixels we can have in one inch of the screen. If we go back to the preceding screenshot with the table where we are showing Viewports and densities and compare the values of iPhone 3G and iPhone 4S, we will see that the screen size stayed the same at 3.5 inch, Viewport stayed the same at 320 px, but the screen density has doubled, from 163 dpi to 326 dpi , which means that the screen resolution also has doubled from 320*480 to 640*960. The screen density is very relevant to RWD, as newer devices have bigger densities and we should do our best to cover as many densities as we can in order to provide a better experience for end users.

Pixels' density matters more than the resolution or screen size, because more pixels is equal to sharper display.

There are topics that need to be taken into consideration, such as hardware, reference pixels, and the device-pixel-ratio, which we will not cover here, as it's out of the scope of this book.

Problems and solutions with the screen density

Scalable vector graphics and CSS graphics will scale to the resolution.

This is why we will use Font Awesome icons in our project. Font Awesome icons are available for download at `http://fortawesome.github.io/Font-Awesome/icons/`.

Font Icons is a font that is made up of symbols, icons, or pictograms (whatever you prefer to call them) that you can use in a webpage just like a font. They can be instantly customized — size, drop, shadow, or anything you want can be done with the power of CSS.

The real problem triggered by the change in the screen density is images, as for high-density screens, we should provide higher resolution images.

There are several ways through which we can approach this problem:

- By targeting high-density screens (providing high-resolution images to all screens)
- By providing high-resolution images where appropriate (loading high-resolution images only on devices with high-resolution screens)
- By not using high-resolution images

As this book covers only the essentials, we will use the second approach, providing high-resolution images where appropriate.

Techniques in RWD

RWD consists of three coding techniques:

- Media queries (adapt content to specific screen sizes)
- Fluid grids (for flexible layouts)
- Flexible images and media (that respond to changes to screen sizes)

More detailed information about RWD techniques by Ethan Marcote, who is the person who coined the term Reponsive Web Design, is available at http://alistapart.com/article/responsive-web-design.

Media queries

Media queries are CSS modules, or as some people like to say, just a conditional statement, which tells the browsers to use a specific type of style, depending on the size of the screen and other factors, such as print (specific styles for print). They are here for a long time already, as I was using different styles for print in 2002.

 If you wish to know more about media queries, refer to *W3C Candidate Recommendation 8 July 2002* at http://www.w3.org/TR/2002/CR-css3-mediaqueries-20020708/.

Here is an example of media query declaration:

```
@media only screen and (min-width:500px) {
  font-family: sans-serif;
}
```

Let's explain the preceding code.

The "@media" code means that it is a media type declaration.

The "screen and" part of the query is an expression or condition (in this case, it means only screen and no print).

The following conditional statement means that everything above 500 px will have the font family of sans serif:

```
(min-width:500px) {
  font-family: sans-serif;
}
```

Here is another example of a media query declaration:

```
@media only screen and (min-width: 500px), screen and
(orientation: portrait) {
  font-family: sans-serif;
}
```

In this case, if we have two statements and if one of the statements is true, the entire declaration is applied (either everything above 500 px or the portrait orientation will be applied to the screen)

> The only keyword hides the styles from older browsers.

As some older browsers don't support media queries, we will use a respond.js script, which will "patch" support for them.

Polyfill (or polyfiller) is code that provides features that are not built or supported by some web browsers. For example, a number of HTML5 features are not supported by older versions of IE (older than 8 or 9), but these features can be used if polyfill is installed on the web page. This means that if the developer wants to use these features, he/she can just include that polyfill library and these features will work in older browsers.

Breakpoints

Breakpoint is a moment when layout switches, from one layout to another, when some condition is fulfilled, for example, the screen has been resized. Almost all responsive designs cover the changes of the screen between the desktop, tablets, and smart phones.

Here is an example with comments inside:

```
@media only screen and (max-width: 480px) {
   //mobile styles
   // up to 480px size
}
```

Media query in the preceding code will only be used if the width of the screen is 480 px or less.

```
@media only screen and (min-width:481px) and (max-width: 768px) {
   //tablet styles
   //between 481 and 768px
}
```

Media query in the preceding code will only be used the width of the screen is between the 481 px and 768 px.

```
@media only screen and (min-width:769px) {
   //desktop styles
   //from 769px and up
}
```

Media query in the preceding code will only be used when the width of the screen is 769 px and more.

> The minimum width value in desktop styles is 1 pixel over the maximum width value in tablet styles, and the same difference is there between values from tablet and mobile styles. We are doing this in order to avoid overlapping, as that could cause problem with our styles.

There is also an approach to set the maximum width and minimum width with em values. Setting em of the screen for maximum will mean that the width of the screen is set relative to the device's font size. If the font size for the device is 16 px (which is the usual size), the maximum width for mobile styles would be *480/16=30*. Why do we use em values? With pixel sizes, everything is fixed; for example, h1 is 19 px (or 1.5 em of the default size of 16 px), and that's it. With em sizes, everything is relative, so if we change the default value in the browser from, for example, 16 px to 18 px, everything relative to that will change.

Therefore, all `h1` values will change from 19 px to 22 px and make our layout "zoomable". Here is the example with sizes changed to em:

```
@media only screen and (max-width: 30em) {
  //mobile styles
  // up to 480px size
}

@media only screen and (min-width:30em) and (max-width: 48em) {
  //tablet styles
  //between 481 and 768px
}

@media only screen and (min-width:48em) {
  //desktop styles
  //from 769px and up
}
```

Fluid grids

The major point in RWD is that the content should adapt to any screen it's viewed on. One of the best solutions to do this is to use fluid layouts where our content can be resized on each breakpoint.

> *In fluid grids, we define a maximum layout size for the design. The grid is divided into a specific number of columns to keep the layout clean and easy to handle. Then we design each element with proportional widths and heights instead of pixel based dimensions. So whenever the device or screen size is changed, elements will adjust their widths and heights by the specified proportions to its parent container.*

Reference: `http://www.1stwebdesigner.com/tutorials/fluid-grids-in-responsive-design/`.

To make the grid flexible (or elastic), we can use the `%` points, or we can use the em values, whichever suits us better. We can make our own fluid grids, or we can use grid frameworks. As there are so many frameworks available, I would recommend that you use the existing framework rather than building your own.

Grid frameworks could use a single grid that covers various screen sizes, or we can have multiple grids for each of the break points or screen size categories, such as mobiles, tablets, and desktops.

Frameworks positives

The key positive features of frameworks are:

- **Faster prototyping**: Our clients can see and approve our prototypes faster.
- **Faster development**: The cost borne by the client is reduced. We can now complete more projects within the same time period.

Frameworks negatives

The key negative features of frameworks are:

- It takes some time to learn the framework rules

- They are usually class-based with non-semantic class names, which can clutter up our code

- They add extra container elements, which makes our HTML code bigger

- They are large in size and that increases the page loading time

Some of the notable frameworks are **Twitter's Bootstrap, Foundation**, and **SemanticUI**. I prefer Twitter's Bootstrap, as it really helps me speed up the process and it is the most used framework currently.

Flexible images and media

Last but not the least important, are images and media (videos). The problem with them is that they are elements that come with fixed sizes. There are several approaches to fix this:

- Replacing dimensions with percentage values
- Using maximum widths
- Using background images only for some cases, as these are not good for accessibility
- Using some libraries, such as Scott Jehl's picturefill
- Taking out the width and height parameters from the image tag and dealing with dimensions in CSS

We will tackle this quest in more detail in *Chapter 7, Working with Images and Videos*.

Setting up the WordPress environment

In order to achieve a responsive design for a WordPress site, you need a WordPress theme that employs the basic techniques of RWD.

In this section, we will cover:

- Installing and setting up WordPress
- Setting up underscores (the starter theme) and explaining why we use it
- Installing the WordPress theme's unit test data
- Installing the Developer plugin

Installing and setting up WordPress

Before we begin with any coding, we need to make sure that we set up our development environment. There are numerous ways we can do it, but my preference is to have:

- Local installation on the hard drive
- Automatic syncing to our server (this step is optional)

I perform autosyncing to my server because my local environment is Windows and my server environment is Linux (CentOS). Through many years of development, I've seen many times that local and server environment differences can cause a lot of headache, so I try to test the code on both while I am working.

In order to make your life easier, I would recommend that you download the PHP development environments. For Windows, there are three PHP development environments that I highly recommend:

- XAMPP (www.apachefriends.org/index.html)
- WAMP (www.wampserver.com/en/)
- Bitnami (www.bitnami.com/stack/wordpress)

These packages will install and configure Apache, Mysql, and PHP automatically for you. Only Bitnami will install WordPress for you as well. All of them are pretty good and the choice just depends on your preference. I use XAMPP as I am used to it.

For Mac OS X, I recommend:

- MAMP (www.mamp.info/en/)
- XAMPP (www.apachefriends.org/index.html)
- Bitnami (www.bitnami.com/stack/wordpress)

I was using MAMP on Mac OS X and had no issues. MAMP Pro is even better, as it provides more options to make our life easier, and it is well worth the investment. When these packages are installed, WordPress should be downloaded from `http:/www.wordpress.org/download/`. After it is downloaded, WordPress should be unpacked (unzipped) and placed in web server's public directory with the project name; in my case, on Windows with XAMPP installed, this is `C:\xampp\htdocs\topcat`.

 Our project, which we will use in this book as an example, is called `topcat`. Here is a great guide in how to install WordPress locally at `http://codex.wordpress.org/Installing_WordPress`.

After WordPress is installed, our _s or underscores starter theme should be downloaded and installed.

Setting up the underscores theme

Underscores (_s) is the starter theme for WordPress. It has been created by the people from Automattic (the company that stands behind WordPress) and numerous contributors. Why is this theme so good? It is good because it follows all the rules from `WordPress.org`, and it really makes our lives easier, as we don't have to start developing the theme from scratch. There are a number of starter themes that can be used for the projects, and I have closed this one as it's really popular and has a lot of features implemented (page templates, customizer, layouts, and languages) in order to make our lives easier.

If you are an inexperienced developer and you want to follow me from now on, I suggest that you go and download the same version of the theme as the one I downloaded from: `https://github.com/dejanmarkovic/topcat_start`. Make sure that the theme directory is named `topcat` and not `topcat_start`. If you want to start with the finished code, then please download this version from: `https://github.com/dejanmarkovic/topcat`. On the other hand, if you prefer to start with the latest _s version (at your own risk, as the code might change a lot further in this book), you can download it from `https://github.com/Automattic/_s/`, or from here `http://underscores.me/`.

The good thing about downloading the theme from the underscores website rather than from GitHub is that you can set a theme name there.

Now let's get started:

1. Put the theme in the `themes` directory. The theme location should look like this `C:\xampp\htdocs\topcat\wp-content\themes\topcat` (on Windows).

2. Activate the theme by clicking on the **Activate** button in `wp-admin`. Your screen should look like this:

   Don't worry, we will soon be changing this flat-looking theme into a nice-looking responsive web design.

3. When installed, the theme's preview should look like this:

Installing the WordPress theme's unit test data

Unit test data fills the WordPress database with sample posts, pages and comments spanning across different post types, image sizes, tags, and categories. It makes our lives easier while developing the theme, as we don't have to add all that content ourselves and we are sure when we test the code of our theme with all that content loaded that we will be able to see if something breaks.

We can test the features of our theme by using the unit test data that is also used by the `WordPress.org` theme team when we submit our theme. It can be downloaded from: `https://wpcom-themes.svn.automattic.com/demo/theme-unit-test-data.xml`.

> More information about theme testing is available at `http://codex.wordpress.org/Theme_Unit_Test` and at `http://codex.wordpress.org/Theme_Development#Theme_Testing_Process`. If you have your own content that you want to use, you can use it. I certainly recommend that you use the WordPress theme's unit test data as it covers all the cases for themes, and the `WordPress.org` team uses it when they test your theme for approval.

Installing the Developer plugin

In the final step in this chapter, we have to install the Developer plugin. We can install it by going to plugin section of `wp-admin` and then by searching for that plugin at `http://localhost/topcat/wp-admin/plugin-install.php`. Here is the screenshot of how the exact result should look like:

Note that the author of the plugin should be Automattic. Or, we can download the `.zip` file from `https://wordpress.org/plugins/developer`.

Now, perform the following steps:

1. During the installation, you will be prompted to choose between three options:
   ° The plugin for a self-hosted WordPress installation
   ° The theme for the self-hosted WordPress installation
   ° The theme for the `WordPress.com` VIP website

2. Please choose the second option.

3. Because the Developer plugin actually consists of many smaller plugins, we should install the ones that we need.

4. I am going to choose the following:

    ° Debug Bar (It provides a debug menu in the WordPress admin bar. In the debug menu, you can view query, cache, and other relevant debugging information).

    ° Debug Bar Console (It adds a PHP/MySQL console to the debug bar).

    ° Debug Bar Cron (It adds a new panel to Debug Bar that displays information about scheduled events within WordPress).

    ° Debug Bar Extender (It extends the debug bar with features such as variable lookup, profiler, and so on)

    ° Monster widget (It provides a quick and easy method to add all core widgets to a sidebar for testing purposes. This means that it will add all core widgets at one place so that we can easily see whether something had broke the layout.)

    ° Regenerate thumbnails (Each WordPress theme has its own image/thumbnail settings. So, if we switch from one theme to another, we should regenerate the thumbnails in order to make sure that thumbnails properties match the settings in the theme.

    ° Theme Check (It tests the theme against the latest standards and practices and provides the feedback.) We are going to use is in *Chapter 10, Submitting Your Theme to WordPress.org*, before we submit our theme to `WordPress.org`.

This is my choice of plugins within the developer pack that I use, and you are free to use others if you want. If you want to change any of the settings that you have already chosen, you can go to **Tools | Developer** in `wp-admin` and change them there.

Summary

In this chapter, we first covered RWD concepts such as Viewport scaling and the screen density. Secondly, we covered the RWD techniques: media queries, fluid grids, and flexible media. Finally, we spent some time setting up our WordPress environment by installing WordPress, underscores theme, WordPress theme's unit test data, and the Developer plugin.

In the next chapter, we will cover the WordPress theme architecture and the purpose of the most important template files.

2
Understanding the WordPress Theme Structure

As we have already installed and set up WordPress and our starter underscores theme, we are now continuing our journey and, in this chapter, we will learn about the WordPress theme architecture and the purpose of the most important template files.

Without further ado, in this chapter we will cover:

- The WordPress permalinks functionality
- WordPress theme structure
- WordPress template files

Setting WordPress permalinks

When users come to our page, for example, `http://localhost/topcat/about`, they usually see the permalink that is set as a post name, or they just see the post ID. It all depends on the current settings in `wp-admin`. The permalinks section can be reached by going to **Settings | Permalinks**. Default settings are always set on a post ID, but recommended settings should be set to the post name because of **Search Engine Optimization (SEO)** purposes. The `about` post name makes more sense than `p=123` in `http://localhost/topcat/p=123`.

With SEO, we are optimizing the website properties in order to make our website more appealing to search engines. With permalinks, we are making our URL readable and searchable by humans. It is easier to find the term *dejan markovic wordpress* if we have a page for it, as in the `dejanmarkovic.com/wordpress` example, rather than `dejanmarkovic.com/page=?123`.

Here is an example of the permalinks settings in `wp-admin`:

Common Settings

○ Default	`http://localhost/topcat/?p=123`	
○ Day and name	`http://localhost/topcat/2014/10/31/sample-post/`	
○ Month and name	`http://localhost/topcat/2014/10/sample-post/`	
○ Numeric	`http://localhost/topcat/archives/123`	
● Post name	`http://localhost/topcat/sample-post/`	
○ Custom Structure	`http://localhost/topcat`	`/%postname%/`

Please note that permalinks in the preceding screenshot are set to **Post name**.

Then again, when the user comes to our page, `http://localhost/topcat/about`, and the `about` permalink is recognized in the backend as the post ID (as that's how the posts are stored in the database), the database will figure out whether the page is of the post type, page, or something else.

Refer to the following figure for an explanation of the steps numbered from top to bottom:

1. http://localhost/topcat/about/ (permalink)

2. http://localhost/topcat/?p=123 (ID)

3. database call

4. page.php

In this case, because the about page is of the page type, page.php is loaded.

 Note that WordPress saves posts, pages, categories, and menu items with their custom IDs in the database system, so the database can check the type of the item by ID.

What is a WordPress theme?

WordPress theme is a group of files (template files) that are working together to display the content to end users. Themes are extensions, like plugins, to the WordPress core file and their purpose is to customize the front-end of the website. They also allow users who have access to the dashboard (usually admins) to customize the look of the website.

Note that WordPress admin themes have been gaining popularity in 2015 and these themes are used to change the look of the WordPress dashboard (admin).

Template files

The `style.css` file is a CSS file where theme information is stored. There are a number of variables in this file, as we can see in the following screenshot:

```
/*
Theme Name: TopCat
Theme URI: http://dejanmarkovic.com/themes/topcat
Author: Dejan Markovic
Author URI: http://dejanmarkovic.com/
Description: TopCat is corporate portfolio theme
Version: 0.1
License: GNU General Public License v2 or later
License URI: http://www.gnu.org/licenses/gpl-2.0.html
Text Domain: topcat
Tags: blue, gray, white, black, one-column, two-columns, left-sidebar, right-sidebar, responsive-layout
```

Let's examine each of these variables. They are as follows:

- `Theme Name`: This is the name of the theme.

- `Theme URI`: This is the location of the theme. I am using the location on my `http://dejanmarkovic.com/` website until my theme gets approved by the theme team at WordPress.org. Then I will move the theme to a location on the WordPress.org website.

- `Author`: This is the name of the author of the theme (in this case, yours truly).

- `Author URI`: This is the author's website URL.

- `Description`: This is the place where we should describe the theme with as many details as we can, because this value will attract our users/customers. As we have just started, I have provided only the basics. I highly recommend that you update this value when you complete your journey in order to make your theme more interesting and unique.

- `Version`: This is our current version of this theme. When our theme gets published, we should change the version number each time we make a substantial change.

 Note that we should not change the version number for every simple change but for each commit.

For example, if we fix the bug, that fix will contain multiple changes, but we will commit the code to WordPress.org only once. Just before committing the code to WordPress.org, we should change the version value.

- `License`: We should state the license we are using for this theme. As we are going to submit our theme to WordPress.org, it should have the same license as WordPress: **GNU General Public License v2**.

- `License URI`: This is the location of the `LICENSE` file.

- `Text Domain`: This is used for localization (making your theme translation ready). We will make our theme translation-ready, and we will cover that in more detail later in this book.

- `Tags`: This variable is where you can choose the tags that describe your theme features/options. For this option, we should only use the tags that are allowed on WordPress.org. Please use the `https://wordpress.org/themes/tag-filter` page as a reference and click on the **Feature Filter** option in order to see the tags. If your theme has the same features as mine, please feel free to use the tags that I've used.

When we complete the settings of our variables, we can see the results by going to **Appearance | Themes** and then clicking on the **Active: TopCat** option on TopCat's area in `wp-admin`, as you can see in the following screenshot:

A software license is a legal instrument (usually by way of contract law, with or without printed material) governing the use or redistribution of software. Under the United States copyright law, all software is copyright protected, except material in the public domain. A typical software license grants an end user permission to use one or more copies of software in ways where such a use would otherwise potentially constitute copyright infringement of the software owner's exclusive rights under copyright law.

> - `http://en.wikipedia.org/wiki/Software_license`

Then, we can click on the **Customize** button in order to be forwarded to the theme details page, as shown in the following screenshot:

Current Theme

TopCat Version: 0.1

By Dejan Markovic

TopCat is corporate portfolio theme

Tags: Blue, Grey, White, Black, One Column, Two Columns, Left Sidebar, Right Sidebar, Responsive Layout

As we can see in the preceding screenshot, the name, author, description, and tags are displayed.

> Please note that we have an image on the left-hand side that looks like the chessboard. This is actually the default image's `screenshot.png` file provided with the theme. We will change this image later on to display our theme layout.

The page structure of template files

Here is a screenshot showing the files in our template directory:

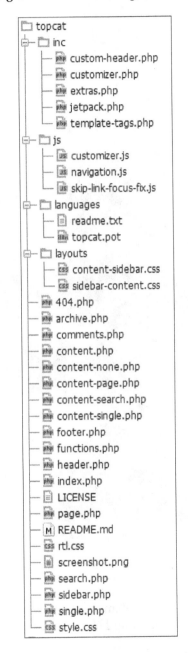

WordPress pages are made from the following sections, which are actually all separate files:

- `header.php`
- Content files such as `index.php`, `page.php`, `single.php`, and so on
- `footer.php`
- `sidebar.php` (optional)

The `header.php` page contains all the elements that are needed at the top of each HTML page, including `doctype`, opening HTML, `meta`, `title` tags, blog info, style sheets, and website navigation.

The content files are scaffolding files, which have a scaffolding code that calls the header, footer, and other files based on the content type.

The footer.php file contains the information that goes at the bottom of your page (closing tags and, in some cases, calls to footer sidebars/widgets).

The sidebar.php file is where sidebar information is found (this is an optional file, as some themes may not have sidebars).

The index.php file is one of the most important scaffolding template files. Its purpose is to show the blog's index page or any other index page. It is also used if the system can't locate the designated template page, such as page.php and single.php, that we are going to cover further.

In cases where we have a blog, we just go to the root of the blog (the index page) and it will load content.php in the loop for each blog post, like the one shown in the following screenshot:

```php
get_header(); ?>

    <div id="primary" class="content-area">
        <main id="main" class="site-main" role="main">

        <?php if ( have_posts() ) : ?>

            <?php /* Start the Loop */ ?>
            <?php while ( have_posts() ) : the_post(); ?>

                <?php
                    /* Include the Post-Format-specific template fo
                     * If you want to override this in a child them
                     * called content-____.php (where ____ is the Pos
                     */
                    get_template_part( 'content', get_post_format()
                ?>

            <?php endwhile; ?>

            <?php topcat_paging_nav(); ?>

        <?php else : ?>

            <?php get_template_part( 'content', 'none' ); ?>

        <?php endif; ?>

        </main><!-- #main -->
    </div><!-- #primary -->

<?php get_sidebar(); ?>
<?php get_footer(); ?>
```

As you can see in the preceding screenshot, we have function calls to `get_header()`, `get_footer()`, and `get_sidebar()`. With these calls, we are calling the `header.php`, `footer.php`, and `sidebar.php` files. We can also check whether there are posts in the database with the `if( have_posts() )` code. If there are posts, then it will call the content template, the `content.php` page, with the `get_template_part( 'content', get_post_format() );` code. If there are no posts in the database, then it calls the `content-none.php` template.

There is another interesting call in our code and that is `topcat_paging_nav()`. This is the call for pagination. It has our theme name, `topcat`, in it. This prefix was added on the `http://underscores.me/` page when I chose the theme name. The prefix (`topcat`) was added to all theme functions and it is supposed to make them unique and avoid causing conflicts. Here is an excerpt that explains this from the WordPress codex:

> *All the functions in your Plugin need to have unique names that are different from functions in the WordPress core, other Plugins, and themes. For that reason, it is a good idea to use a unique function name prefix on all of your Plugin's functions. A far superior possibility is to define your Plugin functions inside a class (which also needs to have a unique name).*

  `- http://nacin.com/2010/05/11/in-wordpress-prefix-everything/`

 More information on this provided by Andrew Nacin, who is one of the lead developers for WordPress, is available at `http://nacin.com/2010/05/11/in-wordpress-prefix-everything/`.

If you want to publish your theme, then you should make sure to change the `topcat` prefix to something else that is unique.

The content files are described as follows:

- `page.php`: This is a scaffolding file for pages and it has similar code to `index.php`. It has the `the_content();` call that calls `content-page.php`.
- `single.php`: This is the scaffolding file that will be used if our `about` permalink (mentioned previously) links to a post instead of the page, and it will load the content from `content-single.php`.
- `search.php`: This is a scaffolding file where search results are shown.
- `archive.php`: This is a scaffolding file that displays archived pages.
- `comments.php`: This is a scaffolding file that displays comments.
- `404.php`: This is a scaffolding template for 404 pages.

- `rtl.css`: In the root folder, we also have `rtl.css`, which is the CSS file for right-to-left languages (languages that are written from right to left).
- `LICENSE`: This file is obviously used for licensing purposes. As we are going to publish this theme on WordPress.org, the license should be GPLv2 (the same as the WordPress license).
- `README.md`: This file is used for project descriptions on GitHub.
- `functions.php`: This is a file where we are able to add our own functionality to a theme that is not a part of the WordPress core. In order to do this, we can also call the WordPress core functions.

As the file is too big for this book, I have extracted the code into small excerpts, which we will analyze together:

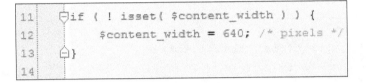

On line 11 of the preceding screenshot, we have a conditional statement that means: 'if the content width is not set, we are setting it to 640 px'. The code for this is as follows:

```
if ( ! isset( $content_width ) ) {
    $content_width = 640; /* pixels */
}
```

We need to have the setup function for our theme and, on line 15 of the following screenshot, we check whether the `topcat_setup` function is already declared somewhere else:

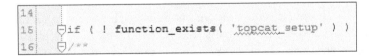

On line 21 of the following screenshot, we are setting up the `topcat_setup` function, which sets the theme's defaults and adds support for some features that we will cover in detail later in this chapter.

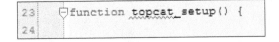

On line 31 of the next screenshot, we are adding support for localization (support for our theme to be translated into other languages):

```
31        load_theme_textdomain( 'topcat', get_template_directory() . '/languages' );
```

On line 34 of the following screenshot, we are adding links to RSS feeds from comments and posts to the header:

```
33          // Add default posts and comments RSS feed links to head.
34          add_theme_support( 'automatic-feed-links' );
```

On line 45, we are registering our theme's primary menu, as shown in the following figure:

```
43          // This theme uses wp_nav_menu() in one location.
44          register_nav_menus( array(
45              'primary' => __( 'Primary Menu', 'topcat' ),
46          ) );
```

 Note that adding links to RSS feeds from comments and posts to the header is good for SEO purposes as we should insert as much information as we can for search engines such as Google to pick that information. If more information is provided, our site will be easier to find.

 Also note that WordPress themes can have multiple menus.

On line 45 of the following screenshot, we are adding HTML5 support for search forms, comments, and so on. This means that HTML5 tags will replace the old HTML tags for these elements.

```
48      /*
49       * Switch default core markup for search form, comment form, and comments
50       * to output valid HTML5.
51       */
52      add_theme_support( 'html5', array(
53          'search-form', 'comment-form', 'comment-list', 'gallery', 'caption',
54      ) );
```

In the following code screenshot, support for post formats such as video, image, and others is enabled:

```
56        /*
57         * Enable support for Post Formats.
58         * See http://codex.wordpress.org/Post_Formats
59         */
60        add_theme_support( 'post-formats', array(
61            'aside', 'image', 'video', 'quote', 'link',
62        ) );
```

> A Post Format is a piece of meta information that can be used by a theme to customize its presentation of a post. The Post Formats feature provides a standardized list of formats that are available to all themes that support the feature.
>
> - https://codex.wordpress.org/Post_Formats

On line 65, we are adding the support for the custom background in `wp-admin`. This option can be reached by going to **Appearance | Background**, as shown in the following screenshot:

```
64        // Set up the WordPress core custom background feature.
65        add_theme_support( 'custom-background', apply_filters( 'topcat_custom_background_args', array(
66            'default-color' => 'ffffff',
67            'default-image' => '',
68        ) ) );
69    }
70    endif; // topcat_setup
71    add_action( 'after_setup_theme', 'topcat_setup' );
```

On line 78 of the following screenshot, we are setting up our first sidebar:

```
73    /**
74     * Register widget area.
75     *
76     * @link http://codex.wordpress.org/Function_Reference/register_sidebar
77     */
78    function topcat_widgets_init() {
79        register_sidebar( array(
80            'name'          => __( 'Sidebar', 'topcat' ),
81            'id'            => 'sidebar-1',
82            'description'   => '',
83            'before_widget' => '<aside id="%1$s" class="widget %2$s">',
84            'after_widget'  => '</aside>',
85            'before_title'  => '<h1 class="widget-title">',
86            'after_title'   => '</h1>',
87        ) );
88    }
89    add_action( 'widgets_init', 'topcat_widgets_init' );
90
```

 Please note that WordPress themes can have multiple sidebars.

We will add more sidebars later in this book.

On line 94 of the following screenshot, we are adding the call for our default styles `style.css` and scripts such as navigation:

```
93    */
94    function topcat_scripts() {
95        wp_enqueue_style( 'topcat-style', get_stylesheet_uri() );
96
97        wp_enqueue_script( 'topcat-navigation', get_template_directory_uri() . '/js/navigation.js', array(), '20120206', true );
98
99        wp_enqueue_script( 'topcat-skip-link-focus-fix', get_template_directory_uri() . '/js/skip-link-focus-fix.js', array(), '20130115', true );
100
101       if ( is_singular() && comments_open() && get_option( 'thread_comments' ) ) {
102           wp_enqueue_script( 'comment-reply' );
103       }
104   }
```

If we want to add some custom CSS and JavaScript, we should use the `wp_enque_style()` and `wp_enque_script()` functions, respectively, as shown next:

```
wp_enqueue_style( 'topcat-style', get_stylesheet_uri() );
wp_enqueue_script( 'topcat-navigation',
get_template_directory_uri() . '/js/navigation.js', array(),
'20120206', true );
wp_enqueue_script( 'topcat-skip-link-focus-fix',
get_template_directory_uri() . '/js/skip-link-focus-fix.js',
array(), '20130115', true );
if ( is_singular() && comments_open() && get_option(
'thread_comments' ) ) {
    wp_enqueue_script( 'comment-reply' );
}
```

In the next section, we are performing the following steps:

1. Adding support to the custom header (this code is commented out as the functionality is optional).
2. Adding template tag functionality.
3. Adding the `extras.php` file for custom functions that are not associated with template files.
4. Making additions to the theme customizer.
5. Adding support for the Jetpack plugin.

These steps are shown in the following screenshot:

```
107  /**
108   * Implement the Custom Header feature.
109   */
110  //require get_template_directory() . '/inc/custom-header.php';
111
112  /**
113   * Custom template tags for this theme.
114   */
115  require get_template_directory() . '/inc/template-tags.php';
116
117  /**
118   * Custom functions that act independently of the theme templates.
119   */
120  require get_template_directory() . '/inc/extras.php';
121
122  /**
123   * Customizer additions.
124   */
125  require get_template_directory() . '/inc/customizer.php';
126
127  /**
128   * Load Jetpack compatibility file.
129   */
130  require get_template_directory() . '/inc/jetpack.php';
131
```

Theme subfolders

In this part, we will cover the subfolders of the _s theme. Let's go from the bottom to the top.

In the `layouts` folder, we have two CSS files, `content-sidebar.css` and `sidebar-content.css`, which are layout templates. In this book, we will use `content-sidebar.css`, as our sidebar will be on the right-hand side on some pages.

The `languages` folder is used for localization (language) files that have the `.pot` extension.

In the `js` folder, we should store any of our JavaScript files. We already have some files that are there by default:

- `navigation.js`: This file is used for navigation.
- `customizer.js`: This file is used for theme customizer functionality.

Since Version 3.4, WordPress has added support for the theme customizer. This option allows the user to change the theme's looks and settings by just going to the customize section of their theme by navigating to **Appearance | Customize**.

- `skip-link-focus-fix.js`: Users of Opera and WebKit browsers that use the keyboard instead of a mouse when click on a skiplink the browsers don't properly move the focus to its target. This file fixes the focus problem in the Opera and WebKit browsers when using `skip links`.

- `skip links`: This is a functionality that we implement on a page if the page has multiple sections. When the user clicks on that link, the page jumps to the designated section.

- `inc` folder: This is the place where we should put the files that extend the functionality of the theme. We already have some files there, as follows:

    - `custom-header.php`: This is the file containing our custom header functionality (this file is optional)

    - `customizer.php`: This contains extensions for the theme customizer mentioned previously

    - `extras.php`: This contains custom functions not associated with template files

    - `jetpack.php`: This is the file where support for the Jetpack plugin is added

What is Jetpack? Jetpack is a group of features and plugins that are used on WordPress.com and can be installed on self-hosted websites. The good thing about it is that all these features were tested on high-traffic websites such as WordPress.com and they are optimized for best performance. Because of all that, they are less buggy too. Usually, if someone has a problem/conflict with Jetpack on his/her website, it's because other custom plugins or a theme have conflicts with it and not because Jetpack itself is a problem. If we need a feature for our website that is covered with Jetpack, I would suggest that you use Jetpack rather than a custom plugin that has not been tested as Jetpack. On the other hand, I would strongly recommend that you use only features that you need rather than enabling all features, as that will really slow down your website.

Template tags, which are contained in the `template-tags.php` file, are actually WordPress functions that we can call in order to have some functionality. For example, `topcat_posted_on()` will display the time and author information for the post. The `topcat_post_nav()` function will display the previous/next functionality.

Summary

At the beginning of this chapter, we covered the permalinks functionality of WordPress. Then we covered template files and the page structure of those files. We also covered the `functions.php` file in detail. Finally, we analyzed the theme subfolders and files in it, including support for the Jetpack plugin and its functionality.

In the next chapter, we are going to start customizing our theme files, such as `functions.php` and `style.css`, and making our theme responsive.

3
Getting Started with Responsive Layout

By now, you have familiarized yourself with the WordPress theme architecture, how to install and setup WordPress, as well as setup the WordPress environment.

Now, we are getting into more fun stuff.

In this chapter, we will get started with the responsive layout and we will cover the following in detail:

- Choosing the right tool for our project
- Setting up `functions.php`
- Setting up `styles.css`
- Setting fonts
- Setting font icons
- Adding essential scripts, such as `modernizr.js` and `respond.js`
- Adding media queries

Choosing the right tool for our project

Before we begin analyzing and editing the code, we should decide which IDE or editor we should use. Some people only use text editors, and for them, I recommend that they use the following:

- Notepad++
- SublimeText on Windows
- TextMate, Sublime Text, TextWrangler or BBEdit on Mac

If you prefer using **Integrated Development Environment** (IDE) tools as I do , then there are three tools in the market that can be used, as follows:

- **PhpStorm**: You have to pay for this tool but it's worth every penny. PhpStorm can be downloaded from: `https://www.jetbrains.com/phpstorm/`.

- **NetBeans**: This tool is available for free and can be downloaded from: `https://netbeans.org/features/php/`.

- **PHPEclipse**: This is also a free tool, which can be downloaded from: `http://www.phpeclipse.com/`.

I have tried both PHPEclipse and PhpStorm. PHPEclipse is a fine tool but it takes a lot of time to configure. When it is configured, it can be buggy as some features will not work. So, we would have to go online and search for fixes, and this can take some time. For example, source control (such as Git or SVN) integration is really good in PhpStorm, while it is just okay in PHPEclipse. I was working on a consulting project and had a lot of problems with PHPEclipse. My colleague, who is working for a reputable WordPress company, told me to try PhpStorm. I was resistant at first as PhpStorm is not free but when I tried it, I never looked back. I just got the newsletter last month from JetBrains (the makers of PhpStorm) and they now have a full WordPress integration in PhpStorm 8.0. For more information on PhpStorm's integration with WordPress you can: `https://confluence.jetbrains.com/display/PhpStorm/WordPress+Development+using+PhpStorm`.

The notable feature that is interesting is the WordPress coding style or the WordPress coding standards support. WordPress has its own coding standards that are really recommended, which are shown as follows, especially if you are planning to create a theme or plugin, so your code can be consistent with the WordPress core and with the code from other developers.

More information about WordPress Coding Standards is available here:

- WordPress PHP Coding Standards (`https://make.wordpress.org/core/handbook/coding-standards/php/`)

- WordPress HTML Coding Standards (`https://make.wordpress.org/core/handbook/coding-standards/html/`)

- WordPress CSS Coding Standards (`https://make.wordpress.org/core/handbook/coding-standards/css/0`)

- WordPress JavaScript Coding Standards (`https://make.wordpress.org/core/handbook/coding-standards/javascript/`)

Note that when you set up the code style, **Options** works only when you type new code, which is fine. There is another option, **PHP Code Sniffer**, which will actually re-edit your code in order to match the WordPress Coding Standards.

If you are planning to submit your theme to WordPress.org, I highly recommend using PhpStorm with the WordPress support enabled. PhpStorm has 30-day trial option and maybe, this time will be enough for you to finish the project or at least to test the tool properly, as follows:

- **Support for WordPress hooks**: Hooks are the options that allow a custom plugin or theme to hook into the WordPress core. This means that the core will call your custom functionality and threat is a part of it.

- **Search on WordPress.org from the editor**: It is a great feature that saves time when opening a new tab or window in a browser and searching for stuff.

- **Integration with WP-CLI**: It's the WordPress command-line tool. With this, you can install, enable/disable plugins, integration, and so on. PhpStorm also has a great built-in integration for JavaScript technologies such as, Sass, Less, Stylus, Compass, JavaScript, CoffeeScript, AngularJS, TypeScript, Emmet, and Grunt. What more we can ask for!

Some of my friends are using NetBeans, and they are happy with it. I just didn't want to spend more time on a free tool when I can use a paid tool that works perfectly and saves me a lot of time.

How to set up functions.php

We have analyzed `functions.php` in detail in the previous chapter. Now, we are going to delve further into it and customize it to fulfill our needs.

In `functions.php`, on line 12, the line of code is shown as:

```
$content_width = 640;
```

Here, we have defined the size of the content part in our posts and pages.

Then, we also check to see whether the `topcat_setup` function is already declared somewhere else:

```
if ( ! function_exists( 'topcat_setup' ) )
```

We have analyzed this code previously, and we should also mention that it enables our theme to have child themes and makes our function pluggable. For example, if someone wants to create the child theme from our theme, they can create the function with the same name in the child theme's `functions.php` file. The function will overwrite our `functions.php` file as the child theme's `functions.php` file precedes our theme's `functions.php` file.

On line 45, we should uncomment the following line as this feature enables the image support integrated in our theme:

```
add_theme_support( 'post-thumbnails' );
```

On line 110, we should uncomment this code:

```
require get_template_directory() . '/inc/custom-header.php';
```

Here, this code adds the **Header** option to the **Appearance** menu (navigate to **Appearance** | **Header**), where a user can add the header image to our template as shown here:

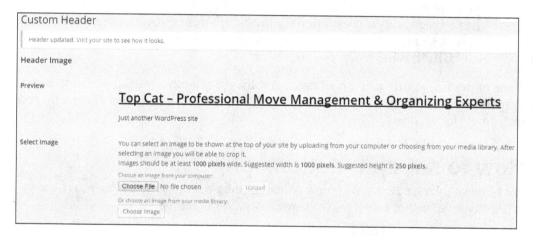

Since this is 2015, we would rather choose custom fonts than basic and outdated fonts. This is why I have chosen two fonts for our use: one for headings (Open Sans) and other one for content (Ubuntu).

As we're using custom fonts, we should load the theme from somewhere. There are two options to consider:

- Firstly, to have the fonts available locally (within our theme).

- Then, to load fonts from an online repository like Google fonts (there are a number of repositories online. Google fonts is one of the most famous because of the Google brand).

Since we are going to submit our theme to WordPress.org repository and our theme has to pass the tests, we are going to use the first option. This option is also a bit better as the local fonts would load a little bit faster.

> Note that fonts and CSS files are available in the Code folder of this chapter, however, I will explain how we can obtain them anyway.

Firstly, we have to download the fonts and CSS code that will assign these fonts to the @font-face variable. In order to get the fonts and CSS code, we should search for the font face and name on Google. For example, one of the font faces is called Open Sans. I found the first result at http://www.fontsquirrel.com/fonts/open-sans. In order to download both, we should choose the **Webfont Kit** tab and click on the **DOWNLOAD @FONT-FACE KIT** button. When we download the fonts, we should put the font files in the fonts folder and the CSS files in the css folder.

> A font should have multiple files, sometimes in three or more files.

For example, consider the following files:

- OleoScript-Regular.eot
- OleoScript-Regular.woff
- OleoScript-Regular.ttf
- OleoScript-Regular.svg

In this case, there are four files for this font.

How do we know how many files should be in our download?

To answer this question, we should open the CSS file attached to our download, and we will be able to see these file names in it:

```
font-face {
  font-family: 'Oleo Script';
  src: url('../fonts/OleoScripRegular/OleoScript-Regular.eot');
  src: url('../fonts/OleoScripRegular/OleoScript-
Regular.eot?#iefix') format('embedded-opentype'),
       url('../fonts/OleoScripRegular/OleoScript-Regular.woff')
format('woff'),
       url('../fonts/OleoScripRegular/OleoScript-Regular.ttf')
format('truetype'),
       url('../fonts/OleoScripRegular/OleoScript-
Regular.svg#OleoScript-Regular') format('svg');
}
```

So, for each font, we should have a separate CSS file with the name as the font name (for example, `oleo-script.css`), where we define it as `@font-face`. In our case, we are going to use one font for headings (`Open Sans`) and two for the content (`Ubuntu` and `Oleo Script`).

Then, we should add this code in the `topcat_scripts()` function:

```
//font for the headings
wp_register_style( 'topcat-headings-font',
get_template_directory_uri() . '/css/open-sans.css' );
wp_enqueue_style( 'topcat-headings-font' );

//font for the content
wp_enqueue_style( 'topcat-content-font',
get_template_directory_uri() . '/css/ubuntu.css' );
   wp_enqueue_style( 'topcat-description-font',
get_template_directory_uri() .'/css/oleo-script.css' );
```

Downloading the example code

You can download the example code files for all Packt books you have purchased from your account at `http://www.packtpub.com`. If you purchased this book elsewhere, you can visit `http://www.packtpub.com/support` and register to have the files e-mailed directly to you.

As we can see from the preceding code, the font for the headings has more code. The problem is that I wanted to use the `Open Sans` font that is already used by the WordPress core, but our theme did not recognize it. The solution for this is to register our own font.

For icons, we will use `font.awesome` and this code should also be added to the `topcat_scripts()` function:

```
//font awesome icons
wp_enqueue_style( 'topcat-fontawesome', get_template_directory_uri()
.'/css/font-awesome.min' );
```

Since we want to build a professional theme, we will also have to add some scripts that would help us add support to the latest technologies of older browsers. These scripts are:

- `modernizr.js`
- `respond.js`

Modernizr adds CSS classes to the `<html>` element for each feature that the user's browser supports, for example, `borderradius`. For features that a browser doesn't support, Modernizr adds a CSS class prefix of `no-`, for example, `no-borderradius`. So, in our CSS, we can target unsupported browsers and provide a fallback using either CSS or JavaScript.

Modernizr can be downloaded by clicking on the desired link on its home page, available at: `http://modernizr.com/` or we can just call it from **Content Delivery Network (CDN)**.

Modernizer can be downloaded using these two options:

- Development uncompressed version
- Production compressed version

It is recommended that you go with the development option, as it will be easier to debug if something is wrong. For final products or production websites, I certainly recommend the production version since it is compressed and, therefore, saves sites or pages during load time. There are many options to choose from and it is recommended, excluding the default options that are selected.

Since we are loading all the local scripts, we should load Modernizr with this code:

```
wp_enqueue_script( 'topcat-modernizr',
get_template_directory_uri() . '/js/modernizr.min.js', array(),
false, false );
```

Now, `respond.js` is the script that enables responsiveness for old browsers that do not support CSS3 media queries, for example, IE8 and older versions. We are going to load it from a local file, too, as follows:

```
wp_enqueue_script( 'topcat-respond', get_template_directory_uri()
. '/js/respond.js', array(), false, false );
```

 Please make sure to copy the code as it is, as there are options with enqueue scripts that have JavaScript code, which appear in the footer. Those two scripts should be in header.

This is the what the `topcat_scripts()` function looks like when all the code is added:

```
function topcat_scripts()
{
    wp_enqueue_style( 'topcat-style', get_stylesheet_uri() );
```

```
    wp_enqueue_script( 'topcat-navigation',
get_template_directory_uri() . '/js/navigation.js', array(),
'20120206', true );
    //font for the headings
    wp_deregister_style( 'open-sans' );
    wp_register_style( 'topcat-headings-font',
get_template_directory_uri() . '/css/open-sans.css' );
    wp_enqueue_style( 'topcat-headings-font' );

    //font for the content
    wp_enqueue_style( 'topcat-content-font',
get_template_directory_uri() . '/css/ubuntu.css' );

    //font awesome icons
    wp_enqueue_style( 'topcat-fontawesome',
get_template_directory_uri() .'/css/font-awesome.min' );
    wp_enqueue_script( 'topcat-skip-link-focus-fix',
get_template_directory_uri() . '/js/skip-link-focus-fix.js',
array(), '20130115', true );

    wp_enqueue_script( 'topcat-modernizr',
get_template_directory_uri() . '/js/modernizr.min.js', array(),
false, false );
    wp_enqueue_script( 'topcat-respond',
get_template_directory_uri() . '/js/respond.js', array(), false,
false );

    if ( is_singular() && comments_open() && get_option(
'thread_comments' ) ) {
        wp_enqueue_script( 'comment-reply' );
    }
}
```

So, make sure your source code matches ours, especially the scripts that we have added.

How to set up styles.css

The `styles.php` file is where our theme settings are set and also where the styles are set. The following image shows you the theme settings that we have covered in the previous chapter; we have a table of contents where each section is shown as styles are broken down into twelve sections:

```
25    >>> TABLE OF CONTENTS:
26    ------------------------------------------------------------
27    1.0 Reset
28    2.0 Typography
29    3.0 Elements
30    4.0 Forms
31    5.0 Navigation
32        5.1 Links
33        5.2 Menus
34    6.0 Accessibility
35    7.0 Alignments
36    8.0 Clearings
37    9.0 Widgets
38    10.0 Content
39        10.1 Posts and pages
40        10.2 Asides
41        10.3 Comments
42    11.0 Infinite scroll
43    12.0 Media
44        12.1 Captions
45        12.2 Galleries
46    -------------------------------------------------------*/
47
```

We will cover only the essential parts that we need to change here.

The Reset section is where the browsers default style sheet is overridden because each browser uses its own style sheets to display the layout. If we load the page with no CSS reset in it, the HTML elements will be styled differently in different browsers, since a default style sheet is used by each browser. By using the Reset CSS, we are making sure that all the browsers are have their default styles set to the initial values that are set by us, as shown here:

```
59        border: 0;
60        font-family: inherit;
61        font-size: 100%;
62        font-style: inherit;
63        font-weight: inherit;
64        margin: 0;
65        outline: 0;
66        padding: 0;
67        vertical-align: baseline;
```

On line 60 of the preceding screenshot, font-family: inherit; and other fonts inherit options. This means that these settings will be inherited from the browser's default style.

On line 61, `font-size: 100%;` means that the browser will render the font size that is set in the user settings of that browser. For example, in Firefox, the default font size is 16 pixels and you can see these settings if you navigate to **Tools | Options | Content**. Setting the font size to `100%` makes our life easier with rem and em values.

The em and rem values

Here, em is the current font size for the element that is associated to it. If the font is not set anywhere on the page, then the default size will be 16 pixels, as this is the default font size for the browser; in em, it will be 16 pixels as well.

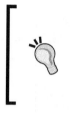

> The most popular method used when working with em values is to set the font size on the body to `62.5%`. Since the default browser font size is 16 pixels, this makes it 10 pixels (without hard setting it to 10 pixels, which wouldn't cascade). Using 10 as a multiplier is much easier than using 16. This way, if you need a font size of 18 pixels, use a font size of 1.8 em.

What is a multiplier?

For example, if we have this CSS code { `font-size: 1.2em;` } CSS code, that `1.2` is essentially a multiplier of the current em value. So, if the current em size is 10 pixels, the list tag is going to turn out to be 12 pixels.

Note that in our `style.css` that we use in the CSS `Reset` section, we set the font to `62.5%`:

```
html {
   font-size: 62.5%; /* Corrects text resizing oddly in IE6/7 when
body font-size is set using em units
http://clagnut.com/blog/348/#c790 */
   overflow-y: scroll; /* Keeps page centered in all browsers
regardless of content height */
   -webkit-text-size-adjust: 100%; /* Prevents iOS text size adjust
after orientation change, without disabling user zoom */
   -ms-text-size-adjust:    100%; /*
www.456bereastreet.com/archive/201012/controlling_text_size_in_should
be together_for_ios_without_disabling_user_zoom/ */
}
```

So, we can calculate our values easily as 1 em is 10 pixels, 2 em is 20 pixels, and so on. The problem with em is that it cascades. For example, if we have the em value set for a list to be 1.2 em and we have a paragraph within this list, the font size for this paragraph would be 1.2 em * 1.2 em.

Here is the CSS code, where we set the font size for the list and paragraph as 1.2 em:

```
li,p{
    font-size: 1.2em;
}
```

Here is the HTML code where we nest the paragraph within the list:

```
<ul>
    <li>list1</li>
    <li><p>list1 with paragraph inside</p> </li>
</ul>
```

The outcome for this is:

From the preceding image, we can clearly see how the second list with the paragraph has larger fonts. That is the result of cascading.

This is an instance where rem comes to the rescue. Rem is root of em, or for some people, it is the relative em size that is relative to the size defined in the root HTML element. This means that if you want to get 16 pixels in a rem value (that is 1.6 rem), set the font size to 62.5% in Reset CSS (as it is in the reset.css file) or for 18 pixels, it will be 1.8 rem.

We can also see some fixes/hacks for different browsers from line 70 through 82, in the following screenshot, where text and other hacks are applied. Comments beside the code are explained through out this code in more detail:

The unspoken rule is that we should never change the Reset CSS and we will follow this rule.

Since the fonts are loaded as we have checked our files earlier, we need to set them for the content and the headings.

We are going to do this in the typography section:

```
146    body,
147    button,
148    input,
149    select,
150    textarea {
151        color: #404040;
152        font-family: Ubuntu, sans-serif;
153        font-size: 16px;
154        font-size: 1.6rem;
155        line-height: 1.5;
```

Here, we have added our custom Ubuntu font in front of sans-serif. We can also see that the font size defined in rem and pixels. Pixel sizes are used as fallback values for older browsers that do not support rem in CSS sections for headers:

```
159    h1,
160    h2,
161    h3,
162    h4,
163    h5,
164    h6 {
165        clear: both;
166        font-family: 'Open Sans';
167        font-weight: 800;
168        font-color: #000;
169    }
```

We have added the custom Open Sans family, with a font weight of 800, and the font color is black.

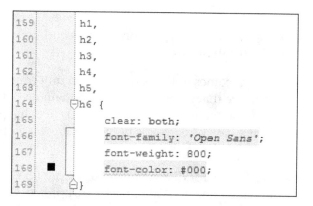

Since the last couple of years, developers have also used **hue-saturation-light (hsl)** values for colors that are more customizable. For example, to define the light value of your blue color.

We will add separate layout files for pages that have sidebar, and those files are located in the layouts folder with the content-sidebar.css name (this means that the content is on the left-hand side and the sidebar is on the right-hand side).

We should add the call to enqueue that file in the `functions.php` `topcat_scripts()` function on line 97:

```
97    wp_enqueue_style( 'topcat-layout-css', get_template_directory_uri() . '/layouts/content-sidebar.css' );
```

This is what the page looked like before layout CSS file was added. Note that sidebar items (such as **Recent Posts** and **Recent Comments**) are below the content, as shown here:

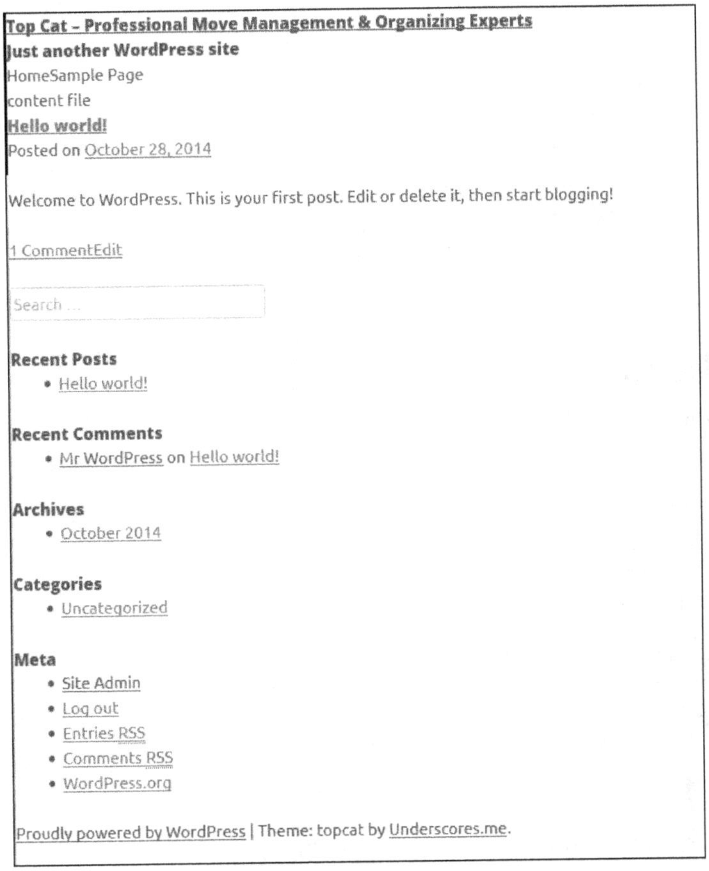

This is what the page looks like after the layout CSS file was added. Sidebar items (such as **Recent Posts** and **Recent Comments**) are on the right-hand side, as shown here:

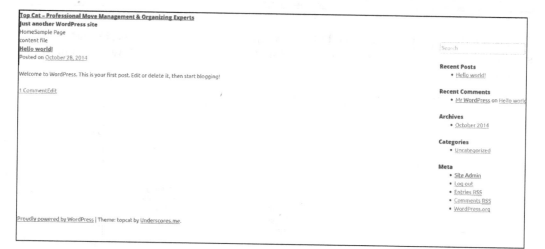

The code for this is:

```
.site-content .widget-area {
  float: right;
  overflow: hidden;
  width: 25%;
}
```

We will change it to:

```
.site-content .widget-area {

    float: right;

    width: 30%;

    padding-left: 1rem; /*dejan added*/

    background: none repeat scroll 0 0 #f8f8f8;  /**/

}
```

Here, we have left the `float` option to `right`, as that is how the sidebar should float. Then, we added a width of 30%. We have also set the `border: 1px red dashed` option, since we want to see what's going on with sidebar (whether it's getting squeezed or not) when we resize the page. We have also added the `padding-left: 1rem` option for cosmetic purposes.

Now, we are going to change the code in the content area. The code here is:

```
.content-area {
  float: left;
  margin: 0 -25% 0 0;
  width: 100%;
}
```

It is changed to:

```
.content-area {
  float: left;
  width: 70%;
  border: 1px blue dashed; /*dejan added*/
}
```

We will let the content float on left, as it should, and we will also have `width` of 70% for the content, since the sidebar is taking another 30%. For testing purposes, we will have the `border` set to `1px blue dashed`.

This is what the template will look like with dashed borders:

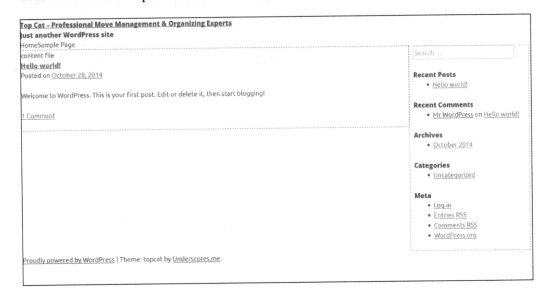

From the previous image, we can see that the content area is takes up 70% of the page and the sidebar takes up 30% of the remaining space.

Adding media queries

Our final step is to add media queries. There are many approaches for this and we will use the simplest one to make our life easier. Our media queries have only three categories:

- Mobile styles (`@media only screen and (max-width:480px)`)
- Tablet styles (`@media only screen and (min-width:481px) and (max-width:768px)`)
- Desktop styles (`@media only screen and (min-width:769px)`)

As you can see from the previous code, mobile styles are for screens up to 480px, tablet styles are for the screens from 481px to 768px (note that there is one pixel difference from mobile styles), and finally, desktop styles are from 769px (note the one pixel difference from tablet styles).

If you want to use a more complex boilerplate CSS with media queries, you can find it at: `http://www.paulund.co.uk/boilerplate-css-media-queries` (this one supports both portrait and landscape modes for popular devices). For now, I highly recommend that you follow our book.

Now, we should cut and paste our content area CSS to our desktop media query, as that is how it should behave on a desktop:

```css
/*desktop styles*/
@media only screen and (min-width:769px) {
  .content-area {
    float: left;
    width: 100%;
    border: 1px blue dashed;
    margin-left: -300px;
    padding-left:  300px;
  }
}
```

When we resize the screen to a tablet or phone size, our sidebar will still float on right-hand side, as shown here:

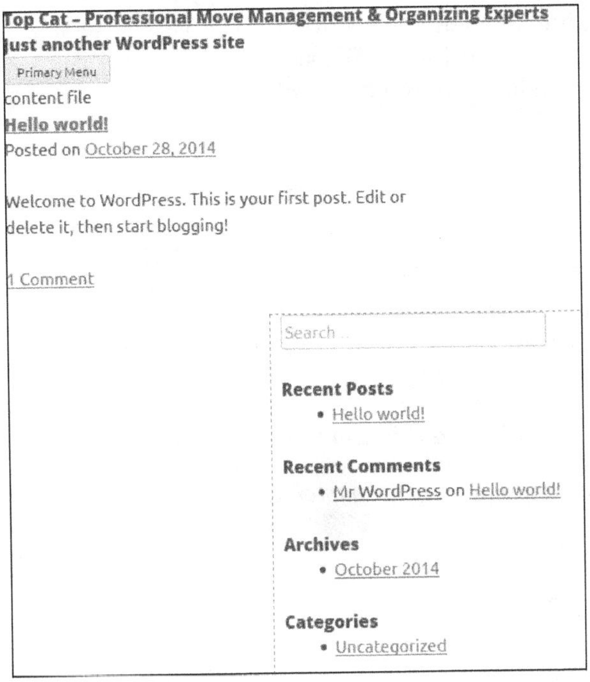

In order to fix this, we will add this code to tablet and phone media queries:

```
/* mobile styles */
@media only screen and (max-width:480px) {

  .site-content .widget-area {
    float: none;
    width: auto;
  }
}


/*tablet styles*/
@media only screen and (min-width:481px) and (max-width:768px) {

  .site-content .widget-area {
    float: none;
    width: auto;
  }
}
```

The `float: none` option fixes the problem and `width: auto` makes sure that our sidebar will only take up the space it needs. If, for example, we have used `width: 100%` (as many people do in those cases), we will have problem if we add the margin or padding, as then our section (in this case sidebar) will go beyond its size. The `width: auto` option makes sure it stays in proper size. The `content-sidebar.css` file is available in the `Code` folder of this chapter, so you can compare it with your changes.

Summary

In this chapter, we got started with the responsive layout, learned how to choose the right tool for our project IDE, set up `functions.php` and `styles.css`, set fonts and font icons, add essential `modernizr.js` and `respond.js` scripts, and add media queries.

In the next chapter, we will dive into the world of header, navigation, and search.

Don't waste any time and start with *Chapter 4, Learn How to Create the Header and Navigation*.

4

Learn How to Create the Header and Navigation

The header is most likely the first thing people see when they land on your website. In today's world where the next website is only a click away, you only have a few seconds to make the lasting impressions.

Navigation is also the key component of every website and the design of the website navigation has a huge impact on results. Navigation is like a road map for the visitors of your website, showing them the way to go through the website and where they can find the information they are looking for.

That is why this is probably the most important chapter in our book. Grabbing the attention of people clicking on your website and easily pointing them to your website information is the goal of every website, and creating the memorable header and usable navigation is something that every designer should do!

Are you excited so far? I know I am.

So, let's start!

In this chapter, we will learn:

- How to create the header
- How to create and style the navigation menu
- How to make menus accessible with `superfish.js`
- How to make menus responsive (making them look good across all devices)

Making our layout centered

Before we deal with the header, we need to customize our page style in order to make everything centered on the page, and we do that by adding a `topcat_page` class to line 22 in `header.php`, as shown:

```
<div id="page" class="hfeed site topcat_page">
```

We also need to add CSS for this class in `content-sidebar.css`:

```
.topcat_page{
    background: none repeat scroll 0 0 #fff;
    box-sizing: border-box;
    margin: 0px auto 0 !important;
    max-width: 1000px;
    border: 1px black dashed;
}
```

The most important parts of this code are:

- `margin: 0px auto 0 !important;`: This code makes our content centered.
- `max-width: 1000px;`: This code makes our content have a maximum width of `1000 pixels`.

I have also created the border to be black and dashed with the `border: 1px black dashed;` code so that we can distinguish this section from others, as shown next:

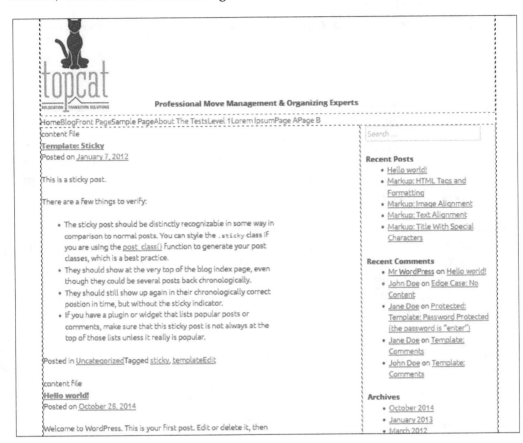

Dealing with the header

Here is the image of the header of our current TopCat:

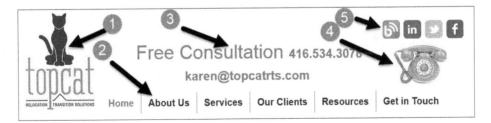

Let's analyze each numbered section:

- Section 1 is our logo.

- Section 2 is the menu for which we will change the look and the structure.

- Section 3 is just an advertisement and the contact information. We will put the tagline (description) there.

 The tagline can be found and set in `wp-admin` by navigating to **Settings** | **General**.

- In section 4, we have the phone image that takes customers to our contact page. We will take this one out, as we will have a **contact us** link in the menu.

- In section 5, we have social icons that will stay in the top-right corner.

As we have mentioned previously, the header for WordPress websites is handled by the `header.php` file. In that file, first, we have an HTML markup that any HTML page has and that is mostly the HTML `head` and `meta` tags. Then, we have the `wp_head();` call, and this function call is actually calling `wp_enqueue_styles()` and `wp_enque_scripts()` that we have set in the `functions.php` file, as you can see in the following screenshot:

```php
1    <?php
2    /** The header for our theme.  ... */
9    ?><!DOCTYPE html>
10   <html <?php language_attributes(); ?>>
11   <head>
12   <meta charset="<?php bloginfo( 'charset' ); ?>">
13   <meta name="viewport" content="width=device-width, initial-scale=1">
14   <title><?php wp_title( '|', true, 'right' ); ?></title>
15   <link rel="profile" href="http://gmpg.org/xfn/11">
16   <link rel="pingback" href="<?php bloginfo( 'pingback_url' ); ?>">
17
18   <?php wp_head(); ?>
19   </head>
```

After this, the interesting stuff comes, as you can see from the following screenshot::

```
21  <body <?php body_class(); ?>>
22  <div id="page" class="hfeed site">
23      <a class="skip-link screen-reader-text" href="#content"><?php _e( 'Skip to content', 'topcat' ); ?></a>
24
25      <header id="masthead" class="site-header" role="banner">
26          <div class="site-branding">
27              <h1 class="site-title"><a href="<?php echo esc_url( home_url( '/' ) ); ?>" rel="home"><?php bloginfo( 'name' ); ?></a></h1>
28              <h2 class="site-description"><?php bloginfo( 'description' ); ?></h2>
29          </div>
30
31          <nav id="site-navigation" class="main-navigation" role="navigation">
32              <button class="menu-toggle"><?php _e( 'Primary Menu', 'topcat' ); ?></button>
33              <?php wp_nav_menu( array( 'theme_location' => 'primary' ) ); ?>
34          </nav><!-- #site-navigation -->
35      </header><!-- #masthead -->
36
37      <div id="content" class="site-content">
```

Let's take a look at it:

- First, we have a `body_class();` call, and this is the function that adds specific classes to the `<body>` tag based on where on the site you are in relation to the WordPress template hierarchy.

> We can pass our own classes by passing myclass as an argument to the function call.
>
> More information is available at `http://codex.wordpress.org/Function_Reference/body_class`

- Later on, on line 23. we have a **"Skip to content"** link. This is the link for screen readers to help users who use a screen reader just skip to content, and not to have to link through the menu.
- Then, we have a site title code on line 27 and site description/tagline on line 28.
- Later on, from line 31 till 34, we have a call to the main navigation (main menu).

As the number one is the logo on our first image, we should start from there. In our code, in the previous screenshot, we don't have the image option. However, we had already implemented a custom header option in the previous chapter, and we just have to add the code for the image functionality to our `header.php` file. This code is available in the `custom-header.php` file, as shown next:

```
9   <?php if ( get_header_image() ) : ?>
10  <a href="<?php echo esc_url( home_url( '/' ) ); ?>" rel="home">
11      <img src="<?php header_image(); ?>" width="<?php echo esc_attr( get_custom_header()->width ); ?>" height="<?php echo esc_attr( get_custom_header()->height ); ?>" alt="">
12  </a>
13  <?php endif; // End header image check ?>
```

Now, let's copy this code to our `header.php` file.

> As I don't want to display the site name on this occasion, I've nested this code in the site name's link code.

The copied code is as follows:

```
<a href="<?php echo esc_url( home_url( '/' ) ); ?>" rel="home">
            <?php if ( get_header_image() ) : ?>
                <a href="<?php echo esc_url( home_url( '/' ) );
?>" rel="home"><img src="<?php header_image(); ?>" width="<?php
echo esc_attr( get_custom_header()->width ); ?>" height="<?php
echo esc_attr( get_custom_header()->height ); ?>" alt=""></a>
            <?php endif; // End header image check. ?></a>
```

When the user clicks on the logo, he/she will be taken to our site's root/index page. Before we upload the image, we should set the image size in our `custom-header.php` file on lines 29 and 30 as you can see in the following image.

29		'width'	=> 150,
30		'height'	=> 200,

> Our logo is located in the `chpt3` directory with the image that has a `logo.jpg` name. Logo's size is 150 x 250, and we should put these values to the width and height options, respectively.

In order to see our image, we have to go to **Appearance** | **Header** in `wp-admin` and then go to the **Select image** option and upload it.

> You can upload your own image if you want, but my recommendation is that you follow our book for now, and then later on, if you want, you can change the image.

If you decide to use your image and it's a different size than what's there in the `custom-header.php` file, you will get the option to crop the image. When you upload the image, this is how your header should look like:

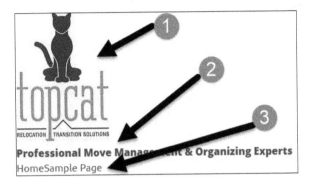

As we can see, section #1 contains the logo. The tagline is in section #2 and the menu is in section #3.

As we can see in the previous screenshot, the site's description (tagline) is under the logo. This is fine for mobile devices, but I recommend that you add `.site-description{ display: inline; }` in the media query for tablets and desktops. This way, the site's description is displayed on the right-hand side of the logo exactly the way we want. As we also want to make the site's description centered on the page, first, we have to deal with the `site-branding` section, as it's a parent section of the site description:

```
.site-branding{
  position: relative;
  border: 1px #008000 dashed;
}
```

This code makes position relative to the site branding.

 I have created a green dashed border for it to be able to distinguish it other sections.

Then, in order to make the site description centered, we have to add the following code:

```
.site-description{
  display: inline;
  position: absolute;
  bottom: 0px;
  left: 25%;
  padding: 1em 0;
/*  border: 1px orange dashed; */
}
```

The `left: 25%` property is making the site description centered. The `padding: 1em 0;` property is pushing it up a little bit as well.

 As I like to design my layouts more in code than in Photoshop and as it's more realistic to me, these values may change later on.

I have also added the test code for the social menu in the top-right corner in the `header.php` file:

```
<div class="social-menu">Social menu here</div>
```

In `content-sidebar.css`, I have added this:

```
.social-menu{
  display: inline;
  position: absolute;
  top: 10%;
  right: 5%;

}
```

We will tackle the social menu later on when we deal with the main menu.

Here is the current look of our header:

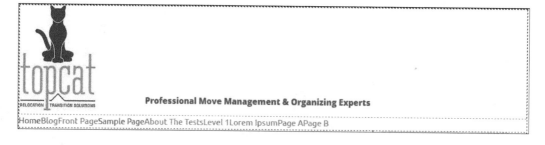

How to create a menu and make it responsive and accessible

Here is the current look of our menu on the desktop screen:

HomeBlogFront PageSample PageAbout The TestsLevel 1Lorem IpsumPage APage B

Now, let's look at our menu on the mobile screen:

Primary Menu

As you can see, the code from *underscores (_s)* changes the look automatically when we change the screen size, but we still have some work to do.

Menu basics

Our main menu is defined in the `functions.php` file from lines 43 through 46:

```
// This theme uses wp_nav_menu() in one location.
  register_nav_menus( array(
    'primary' => __( 'Primary Menu', 'topcat' ),
  ) );
```

Then, the menu sections are defined in **Appearance | Menus**. If you go to **Manage locations** in this section (the second tab in the header), you will be able to change the assigned menu options.

In order to see the menu, we have this code in `header.php`:

```
<?php wp_nav_menu( array( 'theme_location' => 'primary' ) ); ?>
```

This calls the primary menu from the theme location.

Styling our menu

Dealing with the menu is one of the most important parts in the WordPress theme development, as the menu itself is one of the most important parts of any website. Thanks to *underscores (_s)* and its architecture, all CSS classes are already covered and we only have to add proper styles to them. Our menu is nested in the navigation tag with the `main-navigation` class and that's the class that we are going to edit first. This class is located in `style.css`:

```
.main-navigation {
    font-family: 'Open+Sans', sans-serif;
    font-weight: 800;
    float: left;
    width: 100%;
    position: relative;
    display: block;
    clear: both;
    text-transform: uppercase;
    background: #0480b5;
}
```

In this code, we are adding the `Open+Sans` font family (the same font family that we are planning to use for headings throughout our theme). After that, we are setting the font weight to `800` to make the fonts bolder than they are. Later on, we are floating it to the left and setting the width of the container to `100%` in order to make sure that this container takes 100 percent of space. We are also setting the container to `display: block` in order to make sure nothing else goes on the side of the menu. Later on, we are executing `clear: both`, as we were using `floats` (`float: left;`) previously and we need to clear them. Finally, we our setting our text to uppercase as it's a menu text, and then we set our background to our blue color (`background: #0480b5;`).

This is how our menu looks like after these changes:

Now, we have to change the look of our links, and we will do that with the `.main-navigation a` class/selector:

```
.main-navigation a {
    font-size: 15px;
    font-size: 1.5rem;
    display: block;
    text-decoration: none;
    color: white;
    padding: 14px 10px;}
```

In this class, we are setting the font size of 15 px, as it helps our menu stand out. We are also using a 1.5 rem size for new browsers, as 15 px is actually the only fallback value for old browsers. Later on, we will display the block settings mentioned in the previous code. After that, we have the text-decoration: none. We need to use this because our menu items are links and we don't want to have underlines below them. Then, we set the link/items color to white, and finally, we set the top and the bottom padding to 14 px and the left and right padding to 10 px. Here is the look of our menu now:

HOME   BLOG   FRONT PAGE   SAMPLE PAGE   ABOUT THE TESTS   LEVEL 1   LOREM IPSUM   PAGE A   PAGE B

It looks awesome, right? We just set the main level, and in the next step, we will style the dropdowns. In order to see how dropdowns look now, hover about the tests section, as shown in the following screenshot:

HOME   BLOG   FRONT PAGE   SAMPLE PAGE   ABOUT THE TESTS   LEVEL 1   LOREM IPSUM   PAGE A
                                              PAGE IMAGE
content file   Search
Template: Sticky
Posted on January 7, 2012   **Recent Posts**
                                                                                        • Hello world!
This is a sticky post.   • Markup: HTML Tags a

As we can see in the previous screenshot, there is a **PAGE IMAGE** sub link and other things under, as dropdowns are not defined yet. We should change some code for the dropdown in the `.main-navigation ul ul` class/selector:

```
.main-navigation ul ul {
  /*box-shadow: 0 3px 3px rgba(0, 0, 0, 0.2); */
  float: left;
  position: absolute;
  top: 3.1em;
  left: -999em;
  z-index: 99999;
  background: #579DB5;
}
```

In the previous code, I've commented out the `box-shadow` property, set `top` to `3.1em`, and changed `background` to light-blue (`background: #579DB5;`).

Now we want to get the code that will change the background color when we hover over the navigation items:

```
.main-navigation li:hover > a {
  color: #fff;
  background: #579DB5;
}
```

The navigation item looks like this after the modifications:

We are making sure that the main color for fonts is white and that we are putting our background as light blue.

With the following code, we will change the background color in the hover for submenu items, which should be the same as our main background color set in the .main-navigation class:

```
.main-navigation ul ul a:hover {
    background: #0480b5;
}
```

The submenu items look as follows now:

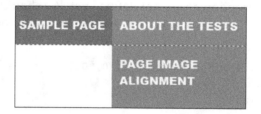

The last part of our code should mark/highlight the current page (the currently active page) in our menu:

```
.main-navigation .current_page_item > a,
.main-navigation .current-menu-item > a,
.main-navigation .current_page_item > a:hover,
.main-navigation .current-menu-item > a:hover {
  background: #579DB5;
}
```

The previous code highlights the current page in the main menu. The following code highlights the page ancestor:

```css
.main-navigation .current_page_ancestor {
  background: #579DB5;
}
```

If someone has highlighted the subpage and we go through the menu, we will see that page highlighted. In the third (final) part, we are applying the main blue color, so if somebody selects a sub-item from a sub menu, that will be in the darker color, and this way, it will be more distinguished from other sub menu items:

```css
.main-navigation ul ul .current_page_parent,
.main-navigation .current_page_parent .current_page_item > a {
    color: #fff;
    background: #0480b5;
}
```

After all the modifications, the navigation menu looks like this:

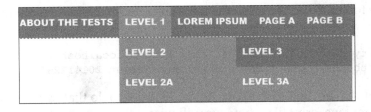

As you probably noticed, when we hover over some submenu and then its subitems, our menu hides very quickly, and this makes our menu almost unusable. In the next section, we will make our menu accessible, and this will also solve our problem with closing our items too fast.

How to make our menu accessible

As we can't access some submenu items because the menu closes too fast, we want to make the menu accessible for the people who use only keyboard, or some other device, so that they can access the menu normally. For this purpose, we will use the Superfish jQuery plugin, which is available at: `http://users.tpg.com.au/j_birch/plugins/superfish/download/`.

Please download the archive and unpack it. There is a bunch of files and folders there, and we only need `superfish.min.js`, which is available at `dist/js` folder. In order to use this, we should copy and paste that file in our theme's `js` folder. Now, we should load that file the same way that we load other `.js` files, and we are doing that with `wp_enqueue_script` in the `functions.php` file:

```
wp_enqueue_script( 'topcat-superfish',
get_template_directory_uri() . '/js/superfish.min.js',
array('jquery'), '20141123', true );
```

> We should put this code above all JavaScript `wp_enqueue_script` calls.

In the previous code, we have `topcat-superfish`, which is the reference name, we have the file location (`get_template_directory_uri() . '/js/superfish.min.js'`), and we have `array('jquery')` — this property says that this code needs jQuery in order to run (there is jQuery dependency). Then, `'20141123'` is a version number (I've put a current date), and finally, `true` means that this JavaScript call should be placed in the footer. So, let's refresh the page and check whether we can find this line in our footer:

```
<script type='text/javascript' src='http://localhost/topcat/wp-
content/themes/topcat/js/superfish.min.js?ver=20141123'></script>
```

We now need to wire Superfish to our menu. In order to do that, we will create another custom JavaScript file where we will wire it to our menu. So, let's create the `global.js` file in our theme's `.js` folder and `wp_enqueue_script` in our functions file just below Superfish's wp_enqueue_script() call

```
wp_enqueue_script( 'topcat-global', get_template_directory_uri() .
'/js/global.js', array('topcat-superfish'), '20141123', true );
```

The code is almost the same as the previous one. The only difference is that now the dependency is on Superfish instead of jQuery. Finally, we have to wire our custom Superfish to our menu, and we do that with this code, which should go to `global.js`:

```
jQuery(document).ready(function($){
    var sfvar = $('div.menu');
    sfvar.superfish({
        delay: 500,
        speed: 'slow'
    });
});
```

In the preceding code, we are wiring Superfish to our outmost menu item, which is `div.menu`. Then, we set `delay: 500`, which determines how long the menu will stay open (to fix our previous problem) if we move the mouse from the menu. The `speed: 'slow'` property is set for the opening animation (the opening of sub menu items).

How to make our menu responsive

Our menu looks good on a desktop screen but we have to do some work for mobile screens. Here is the look of our menu now if we resize the browser:

In the preceding screenshot, we can only see the word **MENU**, and that is not a good user experience. Because of that, we need to change the code in the /* Small menu */ section of style.css, where it says @media screen and (max-width: 600px), which means the code inside of the media query. The current code is as follows:

```
.menu-toggle,
  .main-navigation.toggled .nav-menu {
    display: block;
  }
  .main-navigation ul {
    display: none;
  }
```

This code is making toggle part a block element, and it is hiding ul in the main navigation. So, let's delete this part first:

```
.main-navigation ul {
    display: none;
  }
```

Next, we need to add this code:

```
.main-navigation ul ul {
    display:block;
    width:100%;
    float:none;
    position: relative;
    top:inherit;
    box-shadow:none;
    height:auto;
    margin:0;
  }
  .main-navigation ul ul a {
    width:100%;
  }
```

In the first section, we are making navigation elements as block elements as with the mobile menu, they should all have their own lines. In the second part, we are giving all sub-elements the width of 100%. Let's see how our menu looks now:

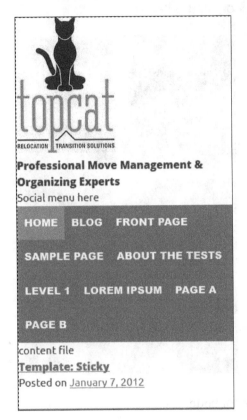

This looks a lot better than before, but our menu elements still aren't in one vertical line as we want. Here is the code that will make this possible:

```
.main-navigation li {
  float: none;
  position: relative;
}
```

With this code, we are resetting our floats and here is the new look:

As we can see, it looks a lot better already.

The only issue now is that if we hover over the links that have children, we have the Superfish animation. So, we should disable Superfish for smaller screens, as follows:

```
var sfvar = jQuery('div.menu');
var phoneSize = 600;
jQuery(document).ready(function($) {
    //if screen size is bigger than phone's screen
(Tablet,Desktop)
    if($(document).width() >= phoneSize) {
        // enable superfish
        sfvar.superfish({
            delay: 500,
            speed: 'slow'
        });
    }
```

```
    $(window).resize(function() {
        if(body.width() >= phoneSize && !sfvar.hasClass('sf-js-
enabled')) {
            sfvar.superfish({
                delay: 500,
                speed: 'slow'
            });
        }
        // phoneSize, disable superfish
        else if((document).width() < phoneSize) {
            sfvar.superfish('destroy');
        }
    });
});
```

Let's analyze the previous code

- First, we are setting a `sfvar` variable to `div.menu`, as our menu begins on this tag (`div.menu`).

- Then, we are setting a `phoneSize` variable that gets the value of `600`, which is the breakpoint for a small/phone menu.

- After this, we are checking whether the HTML screen's width is bigger than a phone screen, and if it is bigger, then we activate Superfish.

- The next code is checking whether the screen has been resized, from the phone size to the desktop size. If it has been, it will enable Superfish, and if the screen was resized from the desktop size to the phone size, Superfish will be disabled by using `sfvar.superfish('destroy');`.

Summary

In this chapter, we have styled our headings, and then we have created our main menu and implemented accessibility features in it. Our menu would not be complete if we didn't make it responsive, and we did that too.

In the next chapter, we will learn about post templates by customizing them and making them responsive as well.

5
Customizing Single Post Templates

In this chapter, we will work on post templates and their components, such as title, meta, and navigation. Single post templates are usually used for blog posts. They help us set up a basic layout that we can extend later with index templates and static pages.

We will cover the following topics:

- Customizing template elements
- Making template elements responsive

In order to understand all these template types, we can use the following image as a reference:

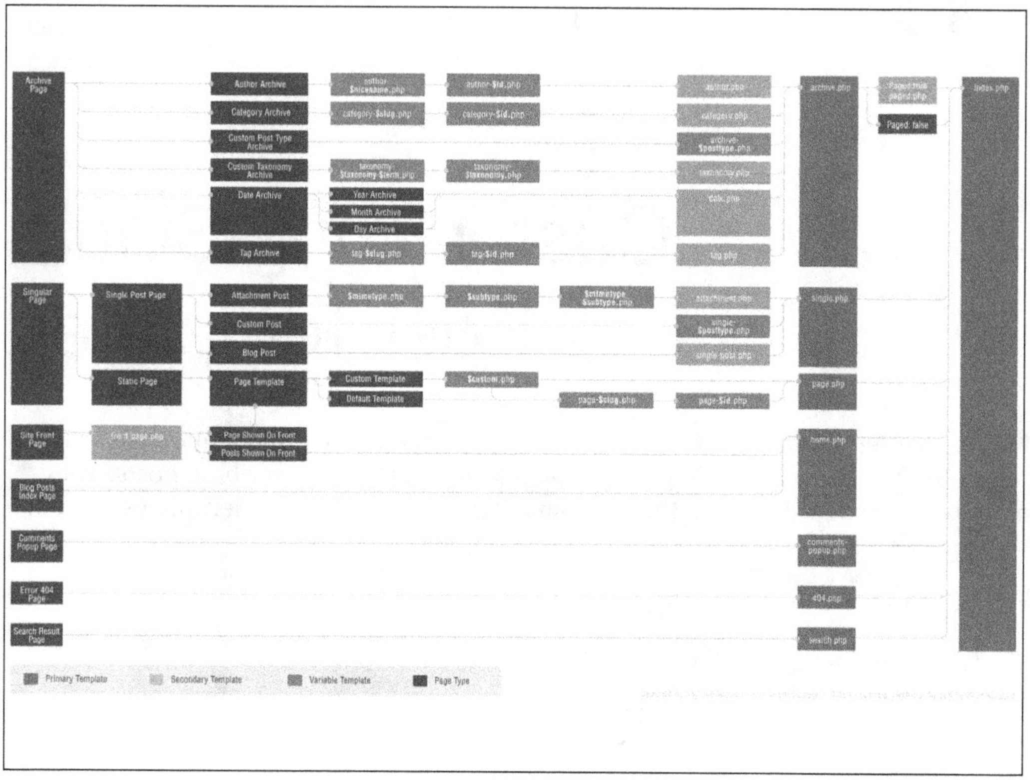

Source: http://codex.wordpress.org/images/9/96/wp-template-hierarchy.jpg

Analyzing single post templates

For single post templates, a `single.php` file is used as a start-up file, and it is only a bootstrap file. The content of a `single.php` file is as follows:

```
?php
/**
 * The template for displaying all single posts.
 *
 * @package topcat
 */
```

```php
get_header(); ?>
  <div id="primary" class="content-area">
    <main id="main" class="site-main" role="main">

    <?php while ( have_posts() ) : the_post(); ?>

      <?php get_template_part( 'content', 'single' ); ?>

      <?php topcat_post_nav(); ?>

      <?php
        // If comments are open or we have at least one comment, load
up the comment template
        if ( comments_open() || get_comments_number() ) :
          comments_template();
        endif;
      ?>

    <?php endwhile; // end of the loop. ?>

    </main><!-- #main -->
  </div><!-- #primary -->

<?php get_sidebar(); ?>
<?php get_footer(); ?>
```

At the beginning of the file, there is a call to the `get_header()` function, which calls the `header.php` file. In more detail, this function typically calls the HTML `title`, `head`, and other navigation elements that exist throughout the site—the items that should appear on every page in the header section.

Later on, we check whether there is a post with the `while ( have_posts() ) : the_post();` code, and if there is, we load the content (part of the page from `content-single.php`) with the `get_template_part( 'content', 'single' );` code.

The following screenshot shows a sample page:

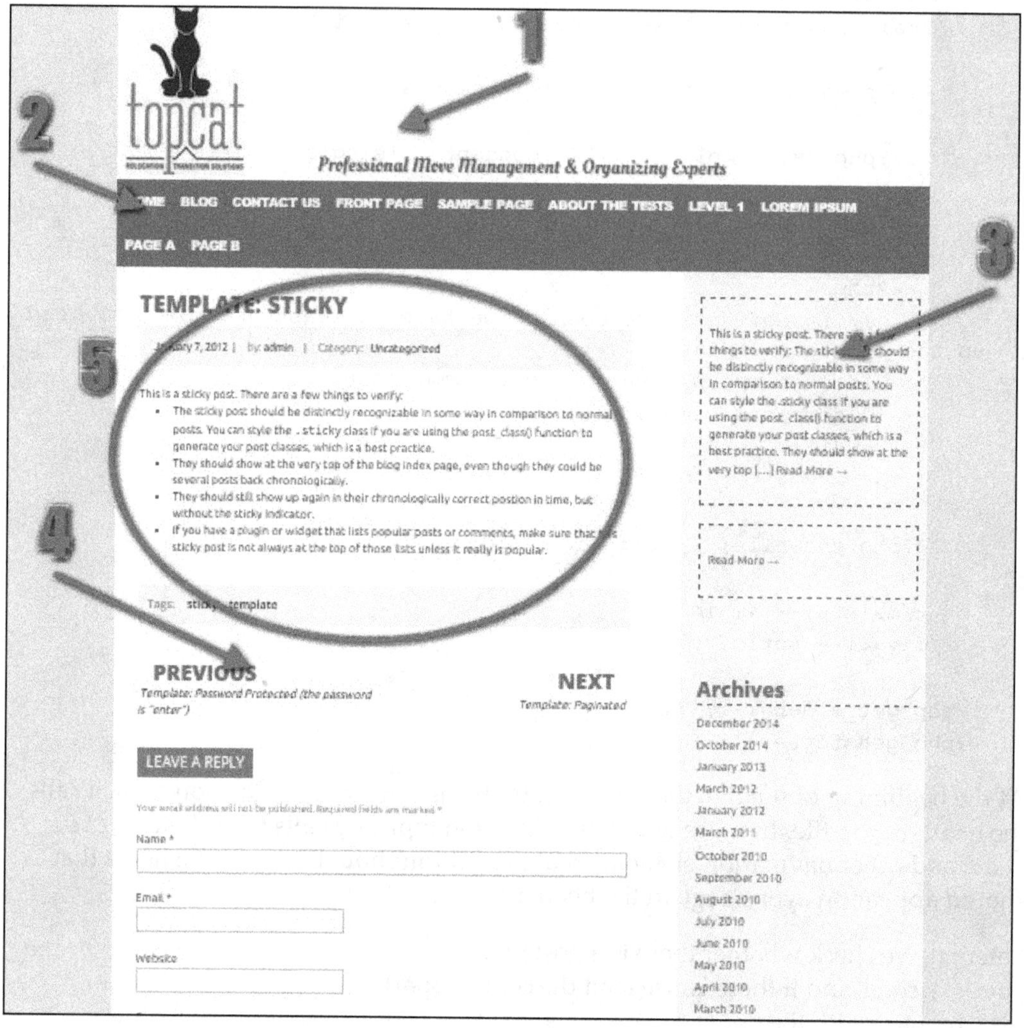

In order to better understand what content is, let's analyze the preceding image:

- The first section (#1) is the header
- The second section (#2) is the menu
- The third section (#3) is the sidebar
- The fourth section (#4) is the post navigation
- The fifth section (#5) is the content part

After this, we load the post navigation with the `topcat_post_nav()` function call and then load comments:

```
if ( comments_open() || get_comments_number() ) :
  comments_template();
endif;
```

If comments are enabled and they exist (somebody has already posted a comment), we call the sidebar and the footer at the end of the code.

Note that for this section, we will use a `Template: Sticky` post. As this is the first post that appears under our navigation, it's easy to manage.

 When you mark the post as a sticky post, it will always load first, no matter when it was created. After it is loaded, other posts will show up on the post's index page.

To make the post sticky, go to one of the posts in the **Posts** section in wpadmin and under the **Publish** section (top-right corner), check the **Stick this post to the front page** option.

We need to click on the **Edit** link in the **Visibility:** section (step#1) to see the **Stick this post to the front page** option (step#2), as you can see it here:

By default, the **Visibility** item of the **Publish** section is closed/collapsed.

Since we are using "Theme unit test data," there is a post with the name **Template: Sticky**, which is already set to be sticky, as you can see it from the following image:

To find the **Template: Sticky post** in our database, we need to go to the **Posts** section of wpadmin and then search for it, as shown in the following screenshot (step#1):

As a result, we will get the post name shown in step #2 of the previous screenshot.

> If we are not sure whether the option is working, try unchecking the **Stick this post to the front page** option, check the main page (if that post is no more the first post on the page), and check it again (now it should be the first post again).

In WordPress, there is an option to enable/disable comments for each post. In order to see whether comments are enabled or disabled, we need to go to our post and then click on **Screen Options** on the header, as shown in the next screenshot:

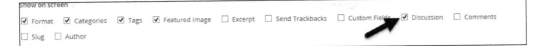

Then, click on the discussion box, as shown here:

Show on screen
☑ Format ☑ Categories ☑ Tags ☑ Featured Image ☐ Excerpt ☐ Send Trackbacks ☐ Custom Fields ☑ Discussion ☐ Comments
☐ Slug ☐ Author

>
> There is also an option named **Allow comments** to enable/disable comments on all posts in the general settings. This is under the **Discussion** section (**Settings | Discussion**).

After this, the **Discussion** section will appear under our editor section, and there we will see the option to enable/disable comments, as shown in the following image.

Word count: 122   Last edited on January 7, 2012 at 7:07 am

Discussion

☐ Allow comments.
☐ Allow trackbacks and pingbacks on this page.

Analyzing the content-single.php file

Now that we've looked at `single.php`, which is the container for single pages of various types, let's look at `content-single.php`, which is where the post content itself gets rendered:

```
<article id="post-<?php the_ID(); ?>" <?php post_class(); ?>>
  <header class="entry-header">
    <?php the_title( '<h1 class="entry-title">', '</h1>' ); ?>

    <div class="entry-meta">
      <?php topcat_posted_on(); ?>
    </div><!-- .entry-meta -->
```

```
  </header><!-- .entry-header -->

  <div class="entry-content">
    <?php the_content(); ?>
    <?php
      wp_link_pages( array(
        'before' => '<div class="page-links">' . __( 'Pages:',
'topcat' ),
        'after'  => '</div>',
      ) );
    ?>
  </div><!-- .entry-content -->

  <footer class="entry-footer">
    <?php topcat_entry_footer(); ?>
  </footer><!-- .entry-footer -->
</article><!-- #post-## -->
```

First, let's analyze what each part of our code renders visually on a single post page, and later on, we will analyze the rendered markup (HTML), too. For this, we need to go to http://localhost/topcat/title-with-special-characters/.

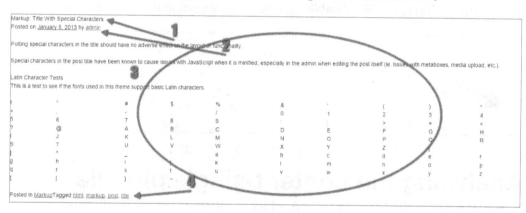

[💡 If you are not working on a localhost, please change the hostname
localhost to the hostname of your environment.]

The following code prints out the post title (#1 in the preceding image):

```
<?php the_title( '<h1 class="entry-title">', '</h1>' ); ?>
```

This code prints out the meta-information for a single post (#2 in the previous image):

```
<div class="entry-meta">
  <?php topcat_posted_on(); ?>
</div>
```

The following code prints out the post content (#3 in the preceding image):

```
<div class="entry-content">
  <?php the_content(); ?>
  <?php
    wp_link_pages( array(
      'before' => '<div class="page-links">' . __( 'Pages:', 'topcat'
),
      'after'  => '</div>',
    ) );
  ?>
</div><!-- .entry-content -->
```

The following code prints out the footer (#4 in the previous image):

```
<footer class="entry-footer">
  <?php topcat_entry_footer(); ?>
</footer><!-- .entry-footer -->
```

Now, let's analyze the rendered markup (HTML) that we got from our code, as there are a lot of other things going on under the hood.

In the first line of the content-single.php file, we have an article tag with an ID and class. The ID is created from the word post- and the post ID the_ID(); the class is generated from the post_class() function. The rendered HTML looks like this:

```
<article class="post-1241 post type-post status-publish format-
standard hentry category-uncategorized tag-sticky-2 tag-template"
id="post-1241">
```

As we can see from the preceding code, there are so many classes that we can utilize in order to reach our goals. These classes allow us to use CSS to target specific post types, posts, statuses, and formats in order to change the appearance of these posts, such as the following:

- post-1241: Access only the 1241 post
- post: Access all the posts
- type-post: Access the content of a type post
- status-publish: Access any content that has its status as published
- format-standard: Access any content that has the standard post format

In a sophisticated software, such as PhpStorm or NetBeans, you can easily inspect the function call just to see the declaration of the function or class. For example, we can right-click on the code on a post_class() call and go to **Go To | Declaration**. Then we will be able to see the insides of the function. Isn't that cool?

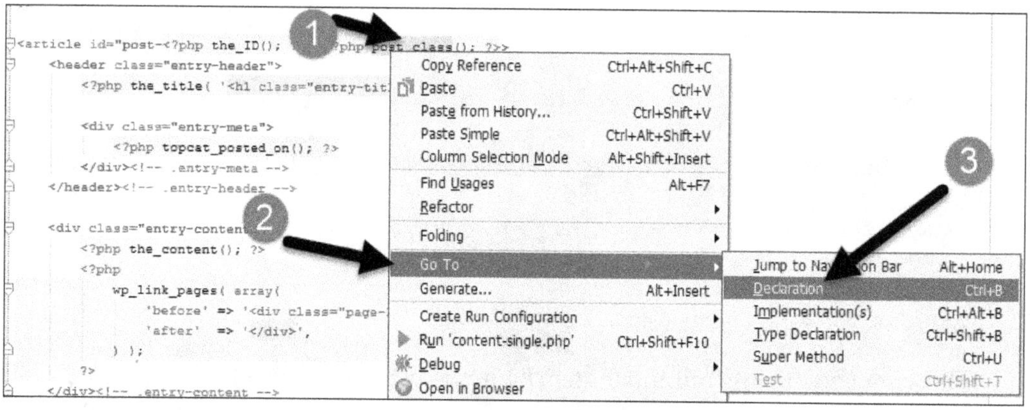

This is the screenshot from the PhpStorm IDE.

Post Format is a piece of metainformation that can be used by theme to customize its presentation of a post. The Post Formats feature provides a standardized list of formats that is available to all the themes that support the feature. Themes are not required to support every format on the list. In short, with a theme that supports Post Formats, a blogger can change the look of each post by choosing a Post Format from the radio button list.

Post Format (if supported by the theme) can be changed in the wpadmin page of each post or page. It can be found on the right-side widget called **Format**, as you can see from the following image:

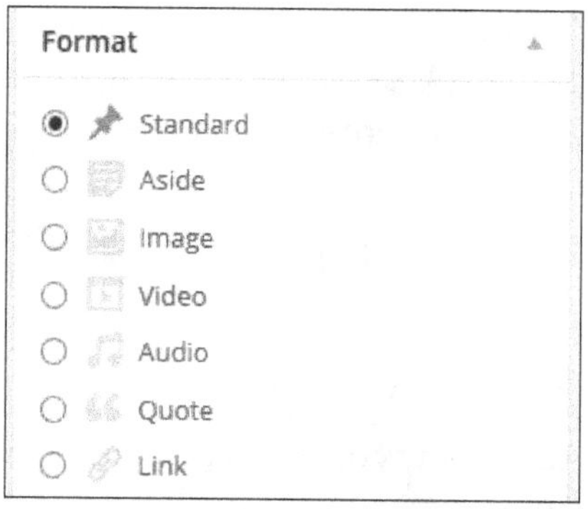

The following is the result:

```
function post_class( $class = '', $post_id = null ) {
  // Separates classes with a single space, collates classes for
post DIV
    echo 'class="' . join( ' ', get_post_class( $class, $post_id ) )
  . '"';
}
```

After code in `article` tag, we have the `the_title()` function, which prints the title on the screen and uses `h1` with the `entry-title` class. Just after this, we have `topcat_posted_on`, which provides the date and by whom it was posted information, such as "Posted on January 7, 2012, by the admin." Later on, we have the `the_content()` call, which gets the posts content; after this, we have the `wp_link_pages()` function that provides the previous/next links (this is the previous/next page of a paginated post).

There are two reasons why you will like to use paginated posts:

- Page views are very important for **Search Engine Optimization (SEO)**. If we split the posts into multiple pages, we will increase page views for our website and our website will rank better with search engines.

> A **page view** (**PV**) or page impression is a request to load a single HTML file (web page) of an Internet site. On the **World Wide Web** (**WWW**), a page request would result from a web surfer clicking on a link on another page pointing to the page in question. This can be contrasted with a hit, which refers to a request for any file from a web server. There may, therefore, be many hits per page view since an HTML page can be made up of multiple files. On balance, PV refer to a number of pages that are viewed or clicked on the site during the given time.

- If we have a lot of text in the post and there is a probability that users will not read the whole post at once, it would be better to split the post into multiple pages. So, readers can bookmark the page where they have stopped reading and continue later from there.

Then, we have the `topcat_entry_footer()` call for a function that is declared in `inc/template-tags.php`. Let's analyze the code now:

```
function topcat_entry_footer() {
  if ( 'post' == get_post_type() ) {
    $posttags = get_the_tags();
    echo '<div class="tags-links">Tags:<span>  ';
    if ($posttags) {
      foreach($posttags as $tag) {
        echo '<i class=" fa fa-tag"></i>  ' .
```

```
            '<a  href="' . get_tag_link($tag->term_id) . '">' .
            $tag->name . '</a>  ' ;
      }
    }
    echo '</span><div>';
}

  if ( ! is_single() && ! post_password_required() && (
comments_open() || get_comments_number() ) ) {
    echo '<span class="comments-link">';
    comments_popup_link( __( 'Leave a comment', 'topcat' ), __( '1
Comment', 'topcat' ), __( '% Comments', 'topcat' ) );
    echo '</span>';
  }

}
```

As we can see from the preceding code, we want to display the tags in the posts (as tags can only be assigned to posts not pages). Our code checks with the `if` statement whether the page is a post or not. If it's a post, it will print out categories and tags. Later on, it checks whether it's a single post page (which means it's not archived).

> Archive posts/pages list or index a number of posts on a page, and usually, they display the post title, metacategories and meta tags, and excerpts from the content. Single post pages display everything mentioned previously, plus the full content instead of excerpts, and comments too if enabled.

Template improvements

We have analyzed the code and now it's the time to make our changes. As I said previously, a number of developers, including myself, now like to design in a browser. This is because when you interact more with your design, you get better ideas and want to improve more. On the other side, you should be careful not to go in the feature creep state.

> Feature creep is a state where you or your customers feel like adding more features, and this road then doesn't end easily. My recommendation is to make changes only if you think they will improve the design and usability of the site, but at the same time, be careful about how many changes you make as you need to finish your project on time.

In our case, we need to finish our theme and submit it to `WordPress.org` as soon as we can. Later on, we can make changes and updates.

Header improvements

I have added a silver background color in order to distinguish the background from the content of the site. This change should be done in the `style.css` file's `Content` section by adding this code:

```
body{
    background: none repeat scroll 0 0 #e6e9ed;
}
```

Now that we can clearly distinguish the sections, we should comment out the borders in `content-sidebar.css`:

```
.topcat_page  /*  border: 1px black dashed; */
.site-branding /*   border: 1px #008000 dashed; */
.site-content .widget-area /* border: 1px red dashed;*/
```

After that, I have decided to give a little space to the header logo that looks like this:

As we can clearly see from the previous image, there is no space on the left side by the border. The solution is to add `div` with the `logo-container` class around our logo to `header.php`:

```
<div class="logo-container">
  <?php if ( get_header_image() ) : ?>
    <a href="<?php echo esc_url( home_url( '/' ) ); ?>"
rel="home"><img src="<?php header_image(); ?>" width="<?php echo
esc_attr( get_custom_header()->width ); ?>" height="<?php echo
esc_attr( get_custom_header()->height ); ?>" alt=""></a>
  <?php endif; // End header image check. ?>
  </div>
```

I've put a `logo-container` class in our `styles.css` file in the new section `13.Header` that I have created:

```
/*---------------------------------------------------------
13. Header
-----------------------------------------------------------*/

.logo-container{padding: 0px 10px;}
```

With this change, our logo image is moved a little bit to the right:

Under the header section in `styles.css`, we can create another section `14.Colors` where we can store our color palette values:

```
*----------------------------------------------------------------
14. Colors
----------------------------------------------------------------*/
/*our blue #0480b5; */
/*our blue light #579DB5; */
```

> The comments are added by me and they don't render anything, as they are here for the information purposes only.

After moving the logo, the site description doesn't look nice, as you can see it from the following image:

Professional Move Management & Organizing Experts

We can change that, too. In order to change the default look, we have to use the `site-description` class provided by the underscores theme, and with this code:

```
.site-description{
    font: 400 24px/1.3 'Oleo Script', Helvetica, sans-serif;
    color: #2B2B2B;
    text-shadow: 2px 2px 0px rgba(0,0,0,0.1);
}
```

As we can see right now, I have added the new `Oleo Script` custom font, which was `wp_enqueued` in the `functions.php` file, as follows:

```
wp_enqueue_style( 'topcat-description-font',
get_template_directory_uri() .'/css/oleo-script.css' );
```

Here is the final look of the header with all our changes:

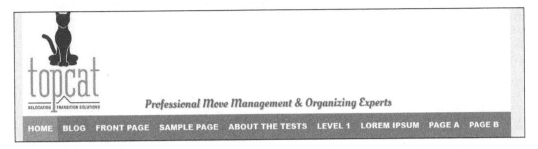

The T size of the font in the content also doesn't seem good, so we can make it a bit smaller in the typography section:

```
body,
button,
input,
select,
textarea {
  color: #404040;
  font-family: Ubuntu, sans-serif;
  font-size: 14px;
  font-size: 1.4rem;
  line-height: 1.5;
}
```

It will look a lot better with all the changes that we are going to do later in this book.

Implementing changes to the post template

We just made some nice changes to the header, and now we will make changes to `content-sidebar.css`, too.

The **Posted on** and following lines are right up against the grey background, as you can see it in the following image:

> Posted on <u>January 7, 2012</u>
>
> This is a sticky post.
>
> There are a few things to verify:

In the `content-sidebar.css` file, I have added `padding: 30px;` to the `@media only screen and (min-width:769px)` desktop media query, and now it looks a little bit better:

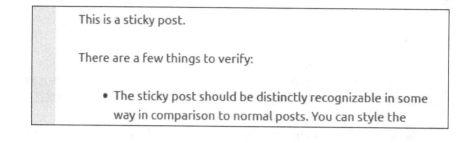

> This is a sticky post.
>
> There are a few things to verify:
>
> • The sticky post should be distinctly recognizable in some way in comparison to normal posts. You can style the

The silver color on the left-hand side of the logo is the silver background that we just put in order to see the difference.

Now it's time to change our post title and meta tags. Here is the current look:

Note that I have intentionally taken a screenshot of the part of the logo and the menu in order to show you how small the entry title is. In order to make it bigger and match our design, we have to add this code to the typography section of the `style.css` file:

```
.entry-title{
    color: #0480B5;
    font-size: 2.8rem;
    font-size: 28px;
    text-transform: uppercase;
    font-family: 'Open Sans', sans-serif;
}
```

Here, we used the color blue as color: #0480b5; and then we have made our fonts bigger by using the font-size: 28px; code. After this, we capitalized our fonts with text-transform: uppercase;, and finally, we made sure our Open Sans fonts were used in font-family: 'Open Sans', sans-serif;.

We also want to change how the title looks in normal, visited, hovered, and active states because our title is also a link. This requires adding the following code:

```
.entry-title a,
.entry-title a:visited,
.entry-title a:hover,
.entry-title a:active{
    text-decoration: none;
    color: #0480B5;
}
```

In this part of the code, we make sure that our title (which is a link too) looks the same in normal, visited, hovered, and active states. Here is the look after the change:

TEMPLATE: STICKY

Posted on January 7, 2012 by admin

Styling post's metadata

Our next step is to style the metadata of the post (Posted on...). This data is in the content-single.php topcat_posted_on() function. If we go to the function's declaration, we can see all the code there. Let's make some changes in order to make the meta box looks better and have more information. From the original function, keep the $posted_on and $byline declarations and get the categories and the edit button from topcat_entry_footer function. This is because in a footer, we will only have to display tags.

Here is the code for the topcat_posted_on() function:

```
function topcat_posted_on() {
    $time_string = '<time class="entry-date published updated"
datetime="%1$s">%2$s</time>';
    if ( get_the_time( 'U' ) !== get_the_modified_time( 'U' ) ) {
        $time_string = '<time class="entry-date published"
datetime="%1$s">%2$s</time><time class="updated"
datetime="%3$s">%4$s</time>';
    }
```

```
$time_string = sprintf( $time_string,
    esc_attr( get_the_date( 'c' ) ),
    esc_html( get_the_date() ),
    esc_attr( get_the_modified_date( 'c' ) ),
    esc_html( get_the_modified_date() )
);

$posted_on = sprintf(
    _x( '%s', 'post date', 'topcat' ),
    '<i class="fa fa-calendar"></i>  <a href="' .
esc_url( get_permalink() ) . '" rel="bookmark" >' . $time_string .
'</a>'
);

$byline = sprintf(
    _x( '<i class="fa fa-user"></i>  '.'by: %s', 'post
author', 'topcat' ),
    '<span class="author vcard"><a class="url fn n" href="' .
esc_url( get_author_posts_url( get_the_author_meta( 'ID' ) ) ) .
'">' . esc_html( get_the_author() ) . '</a></span>'
);

if ( 'post' == get_post_type() ) {
    echo '<span class="posted-on">' . $posted_on .
'</span>|  <span class="byline"> ' . $byline .
'</span>|  ' ;
    /* translators: used between list items, there is a space
after the comma */
    $categories_list = get_the_category_list( __( ', ',
'topcat' ) );
    if ( $categories_list && topcat_categorized_blog() ) {
        echo '<i class="fa fa-th-list"></i>  <span
class="byline">'. __( 'Category: ', 'topcat' ) . '</span>' .
'<span class="cat-links">'.  $categories_list . '</span>';
    }

    echo edit_post_link( __( ' Edit ', topcat ),
'|  <i class="fa fa-pencil-square-
o"></i>  <span class="edit">', '</span>');
    }
}
```

Let's analyze the improvements we made:

1. We have first analyzed the PHP and HTML code, and later on, we have analyzed the CSS attached to this code. In the beginning, we processed the date/time code that is displayed on the **posted on** section.

2. Then, we have declared the `$posted_on` variable. We took off the `Posted on` words, as there is no point in having them there. `<i class="fa fa-calendar"></i>` is the code where we use *font awesome* icons, and in this case, we used a calendar icon.

3. After the `$posted_on` variable, we have a `$byline` declaration, and here, we printed the author information together again with `<i class="fa fa-user">`, which is a font awesome icon for the user.

4. In the third section, we outputted categories; before doing this, we had to check whether our post is a type post. If it is a type post, then we get a category or a list of categories that are assigned to this post with `get_the_category_list()`.

5. After this, we have checked whether the list has returned categories and whether the post has more than one category with `topcat_categorized_blog()`. If the post has one or more categories associated with it, we print them out, again with `<i class="fa fa-th-list">`, which is a font awesome icon for a list, and I've seen it as a proper icon for the categories.

 Note that you can put icons of your choice for this; although, again, I will recommend that you follow the book and make your changes later on.

At the end of the function, we have a code for the edit post link with `<i class="fa fa-pencil-square-o">`, which is a font awesome icon for editing. Now, we are going to make some CSS changes.

Since we have already analyzed the markup and PHP code, let's see what we did with CSS in order to accomplish our new look. As the post's meta has its own container, `<div class="entry-meta">`, we have edited it first in `style.css` file, and edited code is in the posts and pages section:

```
.entry-meta, .tags-links {
    background: none repeat scroll 0 0 #F8F8F8;;
    border-radius: 3px;
    margin: 12px 0 24px;
    overflow: hidden;
    padding: 5px 12px;
}
```

```
.entry-meta span{
font-size: 13px;;
font-size: 1.3rem;

    margin: 0 6px 0 0;
    padding: 0;

}
```

Here, we have first defined a silver background by using `background: none repeat scroll 0 0 #F8F8F8;`, `border-radius`, `margin`, `overflow`, and `padding`. Then, for the child-element span, we have defined a font size margin and padding. After this, we have defined the styles for entry meta links, the author, and category links, as well as the tags that we have used in the footer of the post (we will cover this later):

```
.entry-meta a,
.entry-meta a:visited,
.entry-meta a:hover,
.entry-meta a:active
.author a,
.cat-links,
.tags-links a,
.tags-links a:visited
.tags-links a:hover,
.tags-links a:active
{
    color: #000;
    line-height: 2.8;
    text-decoration: none;
}
```

Then, we have the `.byline` and `.tag-links` classes to set the default color as silver:

```
.byline, .tags-links { color: #999;}
```

As the last step, we will color our font awesome icons in blue:

```
.fa-calendar, .fa-user, .fa-th-list, .fa-pencil-square-o, .fa-tag{color: #0480B5;}
```

After the changes, this is how it all looks:

It looks pretty good now, right?

Content section

It doesn't look nice how the content is separated from the sidebar, as there is a lot of empty space in between:

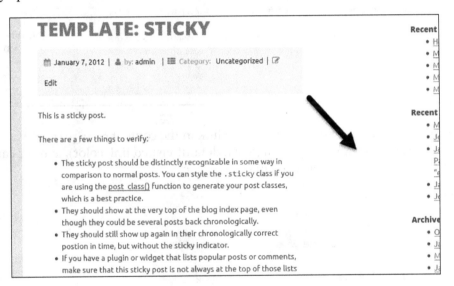

To fix this, we should change the right margin in the `.site-main` class from:

```
.site-main {
  margin: 0 25% 0 0;
}
```

To:

```
.site-main {
  margin: 0 5% 0 0;
}
```

The `.site-main` class is located in `content-sidebar.css`.

Now the content looks a lot better, as you can see it here:

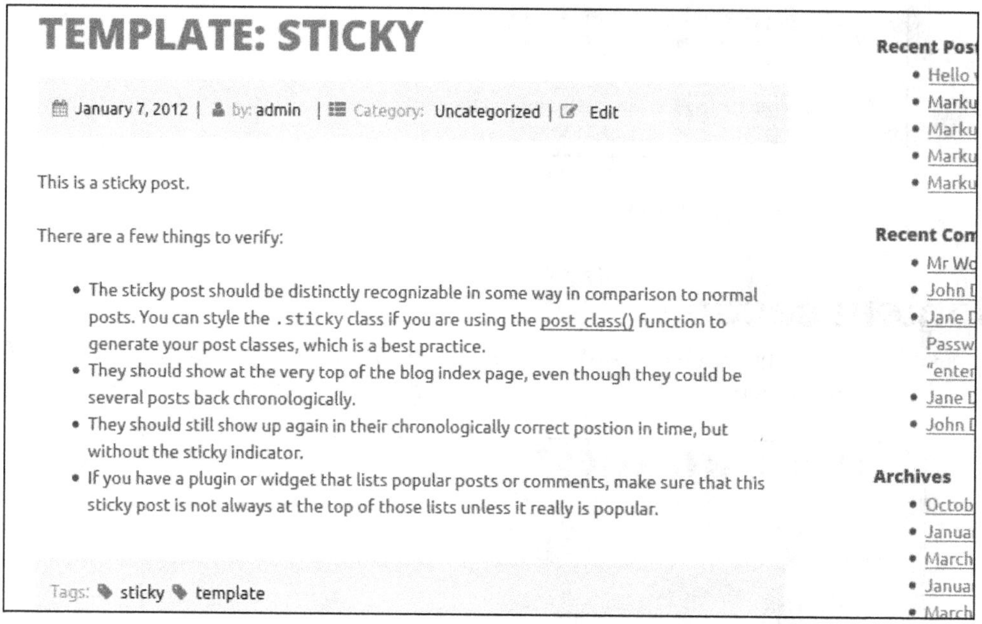

As we can see from the previous image, the link in the content `post_class()` function doesn't look appealing at all (just a default visited link color), and we can change this with only a simple code in `style.css`:

```
.entry-content a,
.entry-content a:visited
.entry-content a:hover,
.entry-content a:active
{
    color: #0480B5;
    line-height: 1.6;
    text-decoration: none;
}
```

Here is what it looks like after our changes:

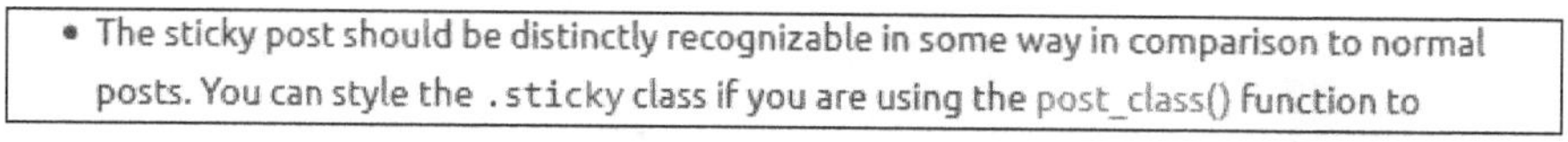

The `post_class()` link is in our blue color now and it's not underlined.

Now, if we just go back to the index page by clicking on the **Home** link in the menu and then go to the post with the name **Markup: HTML Tags and Formatting**, we will see more HTML elements that we can style.

 This post and all the other posts/content in our project don't come with WordPress by default. We have loaded them by importing the **Theme Unit Test Data** from `http://codex.wordpress.org/Theme_Unit_Test`.

We will cover only some of them here, as there are so many of them. This is the look of our current headings:

Headings

Header one

Header two

Header three

Header four

Header five

Header six

If we go to the typography (2.0) section of `style.css`, we will be able to see some headings we have already defined:

```
h1,
h2,
h3,
h4,
h5,
h6 {
    clear: both;
    font-family: 'Open Sans';
    font-weight: 800;
    color: #0480B5;
}
```

We should change the color to our blue (`color: #0480B5;`) to make everything the same, then we can style all the heading sizes separately:

```
h1{
    font-size: 28px;
    font-size: 2.8rem;
}

h2{
```

```
        font-size: 24px;
        font-size: 2.4rem;
    }
h3 {
        font-size: 20px;
        font-size: 2.0rem;
    }
h4 {
        font-size: 18px;
        font-size: 1.8rem;
    }
h5 {
        font-size: 16px;
        font-size: 1.6rem;
    }
h6 {
        font-size: 14px;
        font-size: 1.4rem;
    }
```

Here is the new look of our headings:

Under headings, we have a Blockquote that looks pretty basic:

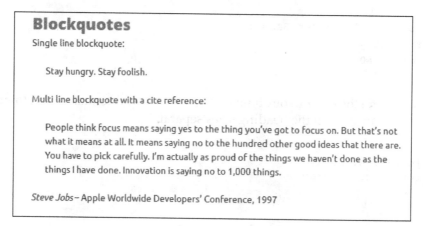

So here, we will first define margin and padding and also add the dotted border at the top and bottom of the blockquote:

```
blockquote {
    margin: 1.5rem 1.5rem;;
    border-top: dotted 1px #999;
    border-bottom: dotted 1px #999;
    padding: 1em;
}
```

After this, we will style the p tag nested in `blockquote`:

```
blockquote p{
    font-style: italic;
    margin-bottom: auto;
}
```

We've made the fonts italic, and since the p element has some strange margin bottom, we have done a reset it here with `margin-bottom: auto;`.

We also want to make the author in the `cite` tag more visible; we can do this with:

```
cite{
    font-weight: 600;
}
```

Since the citation is not nested in `blockquote` but in the next p tag, we would like to align it to the right:

```
blockquote + p{
    width: 100%;
    text-align: right;
}
```

Here is the look after all these changes:

Blockquotes
Single line blockquote:

Stay hungry. Stay foolish.

Multi line blockquote with a cite reference:

People think focus means saying yes to the thing you've got to focus on. But that's not what it means at all. It means saying no to the hundred other good ideas that there are. You have to pick carefully. I'm actually as proud of the things we haven't done as the things I have done. Innovation is saying no to 1,000 things.

Steve Jobs – Apple Worldwide Developers' Conference, 1997

There are a number of HTML tags to style here, and since we have covered the basics and because it will take a lot of time to cover them all, we are going to move to the next part, that is, tags.

Tags

We have decided to display tags in a box just after the content.

In the last part of this chapter, we are going to work on navigation in post templates, and the code for this is located in the `topcat_entry_footer()` function, which is also located in the `template-tags.php` file.

 `Topcat_entry_footer()` is the function that handles the footer for a single post, not a website footer.

I have changed the tag functionality with my own solution in the `topcat_entry_footer()` function of the `template-tags.php` file, and it looks like this:

```
if ( 'post' == get_post_type() ) {
  $posttags = get_the_tags();
  echo '<div class="tags-links">Tags:<span>  ';
  if ($posttags) {
    foreach($posttags as $tag) {
      echo '<i class=" fa fa-tag"></i>  ' .
        '<a  href="' . get_tag_link($tag->term_id) . '">' .
        $tag->name . '</a>  ' ;
    }
  }
  echo '</span><div>';
}
```

At first, we have checked whether the page is of type post, and then, we have loaded the tags in the `$posttags` variable with the `get_the_tags()` function. After this, we are looping trough the tags with the `foreach` loop as `foreach($posttags as $tag)`, and in front of every tag, we have displayed a font awesome tag icon with the `<i class=" fa fa-tag"></i>` markup.

The `.tags-links` section has the same styles as that of `.entry-meta`:

```
.entry-meta, .tags-links {
    background: none repeat scroll 0 0 #f8f8f8;
    border-radius: 3px;
    margin: 12px 0 24px;
```

```
    overflow: hidden;
    padding: 5px 12px;
}
```

We are also styling the links inside the `.tags-links` section with the same styles as the styles for `.entry-meta` links:

```
.entry-meta a,
.entry-meta a:visited,
.entry-meta a:hover,
.entry-meta a:active
.author a,
.cat-links,
.tags-links a,
.tags-links a:visited
.tags-links a:hover,
.tags-links a:active
{
    color: #000;
    line-height: 2.8;
    text-decoration: none;
}
```

Finally, we will color `.tags-links` with the same markup as that of `.byline`:

```
.byline, .tags-links { color: #999;}
```

Here is the final look of the **Tags:** section:

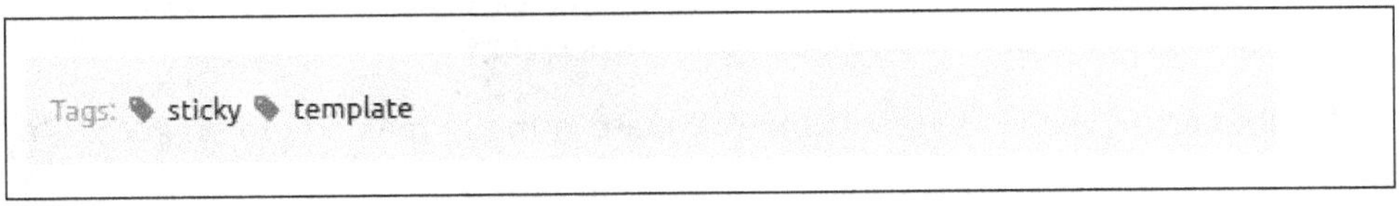

Tags: ● sticky ● template

Post navigation

As I have said previously, the final part in this chapter is post navigation or previous/next navigation. If we go to the `single.php` file and `topcat_post_nav()` function call, we will see this is the call to post navigation. This function is part of underscores theme and it's declared in the `template-tags.php` file:

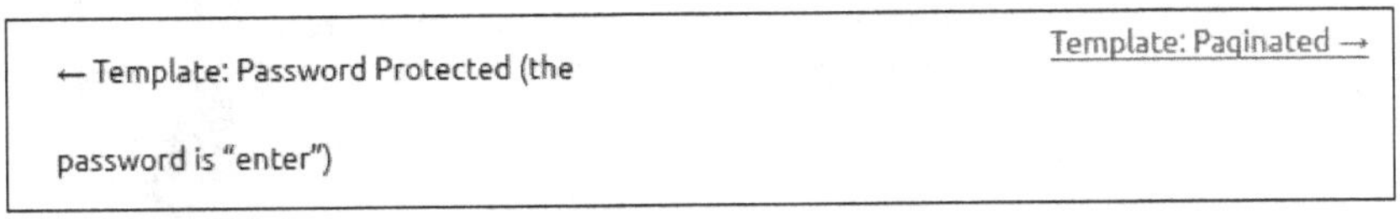

← Template: Password Protected (the

Template: Paginated →

password is "enter")

As we can see, it looks pretty basic, but we are going to improve it. Here is the changed PHP code:

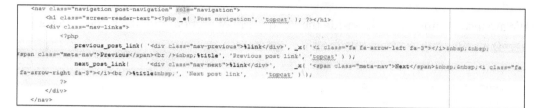

Let's analyze the changed code:

- The first part of the code was changed in the `previous_post_link()` function, where I added a font awesome markup, namely `<i class="fa fa-arrow-left fa-3">` for the left arrow. Later on, we have changed the words from the `Previous post link` to `Previous` and added a `<br />` tag after it. We have also applied the same changes to `previous_post_link()`, too.

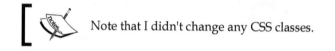

Note that I didn't change any CSS classes.

After this, all other changes that we are going to do are in `styles.css` file.

Firstly, we will add `.fa-arrow-left` and `.fa-arrow-right` to the line where all font awesome icons are being colored in our blue color:

```
.fa-calendar, .fa-user, .fa-th-list, .fa-pencil-square-o, .fa-tag,
.fa-arrow-left, .fa-arrow-right{color: #0480B5;}
```

Because these arrow icons are really small, we are going to make them bigger with this code:

```
.fa-3
{
    font-size: 26px !important;
    font-size: 2.6rem !important;

}
```

Note that I have added a `.fa-3` class in the font awesome markup.

After this, we need to make all the fonts in the `.nav-previous` and `.nav-next` sections black and italic respectively. We are doing this because the titles of the next and previous blog posts need to be in this specific style in order to be identifiable:

```css
.nav-previous,
.nav-next,
.nav-previous a,
.nav-next a,
.nav-previous a:visited,
.nav-previous a:hover,
.nav-previous a:active,
.nav-next a:visited,
.nav-next a:hover,
.nav-next a:active
{
    color: #000;
    font-style: italic;
}
```

Then, we need to style the Next and Prev words:

```css
.meta-nav,
.meta-nav a,
.meta-nav a:visited,
.meta-nav a:hover,
.meta-nav a:active
{
    color: #0480b5;
    font-family: "Open Sans",sans-serif;
    font-size: 26px;;
    font-size: 2.6rem !important;
    line-height: 26px;
    text-transform: uppercase;
    font-weight: 800;
    padding: 10px;
    font-style: normal;
}
```

As we can see in the preceding code, we've colored the words in blue; then, we have assigned to them a proper font and font size, and much more.

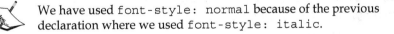

> We have used `font-style: normal` because of the previous declaration where we used `font-style: italic`.

Finally, with the following code, we are making sure that none of our links in this section are underlined:

```
.nav-links a,
.nav-links a:visited
.nav-links a:hover,
.nav-links a:active
{
    text-decoration: none;
}
```

Here is the final look of our work:

Summary

In this chapter, we have focused on a single blog post page—starting from the top, working down through title and meta, then the content's HTML tags, and eventually to the footer of a single post. To accomplish all these changes, we have worked with the `single.php`, `content-single.php`, `template-tags.php`, `styles.css`, `functions.php`, and `header.php` files.

In the next chapter, we will work on the items that appear in the sidebar (widgets), and we will change the way comments appear in posts.

6

Responsive Widgets, Footer, and Comments

As we are going to cover a lot of things in this chapter, we will break it into two sections. This way, it will be much more interesting and easier for you to understand. But, don't worry; it will be a lot of fun, and at the same time, you will learn a lot about widgets, the footer, and comments.

Without wasting any time, let's see what we will cover in this chapter.

In the first section, we will:

- Learn more about widgets
- Learn how to customize these widgets
- Learn more about sidebars and how to style them
- Learn how to edit the footer
- Learn how to make our widgets responsive

In the second section, we will:

- Learn more about comments and how to customize them

Widgets

Widgets are small sections or containers that provide some type of functionality to our website. Basically, widgets get deployed into sidebars, which we are going to examine in just a moment. WordPress provides a number of widgets by default, and many plugins define additional widgets; even themes can define widgets. Widgets can be, for example, lists of tags, categories, latest posts, contact forms, or Twitter timelines.

As we can see, they can be almost anything. When we create widgets in a code, they appear in the **Widgets** section under **Appearance**, where we can select the widget that we like. We can also add it to any sidebar that we want, as a single theme can have a number of sidebars.

In the previous image, we have first chosen a calendar widget, (#1) and then decided to add it to the sidebar by clicking on the **Add Widget** option (#2). With this, the calendar widget will be added to the sidebar (#3). Instead of doing it this way, we can simply drag and drop the widget on the sidebar. As soon as we add the widget to the sidebar, we have the option to customize it, too:

Since widgets are separate programs/features, the options available to customize the widgets depend on the code that creates the widget.

In this case, as seen in the preceding image, we have the option to add the title.

Some widgets may not have the option to be customized.

Sidebars

Sidebars are areas that are actually containers for our widgets. A few years ago, when they were first built, they were used for the left and right sidebars; that's why they have this name. Sidebar containers have evolved so much, and now they can be placed anywhere you want them to be: on the left or right side, in the header or footer, and even in the post content area. Sidebar containers are usually defined in the functions.php file using the register_sidebar() function, and this is also the case in our example:

```
/**
 * Register widget area.
 *
 * @link http://codex.wordpress.org/Function_Reference/register_sidebar
 */
function topcat_widgets_init() {
    register_sidebar( array(
        'name'          => __( 'Sidebar', 'topcat' ),
        'id'            => 'sidebar-1',
        'description'   => '',
        'before_widget' => '<aside id="%1$s" class="widget %2$s">',
        'after_widget'  => '</aside>',
        'before_title'  => '<h1 class="widget-title">',
        'after_title'   => '</h1>',
    ) );
}
add_action( 'widgets_init', 'topcat_widgets_init' );
```

 More information about the register_sidebar() function can be found in *Appendix, Submitting Your Theme to WordPress.org* of our book or in it's Codex page at http://codex.wordpress.org/Function_Reference/register_sidebar.

As we can see from the preceding image, we have a function call to `topcat_widgets_init()`, which is later on called with the `add_action( 'widgets_init', 'topcat_widgets_init')`; hook. This means that this function is being triggered with the `widget_init` function. As we can also see from the preceding code, in the `register_sidebar()` function, we are setting the following:

- `name`

- `id`

- `description` (which is currently empty)

- `before_widget` and `after_widget` (where our widgets are going to be nested in, for example, the `<aside>` tag)

- `before-title` and `after-title` (where our title is going to be nested)

Since, for our theme, we want to have more than one sidebar, we will create another one (the footer sidebar) in the same function, just under the first `register_sidebar()` code:

```
function topcat_widgets_init() {
    register_sidebar( array(
        'name'          => __( 'Sidebar', 'topcat' ),
        'id'            => 'sidebar-1',
        'description'   => '',
        'before_widget' => '<aside id="%1$s" class="widget %2$s">',
        'after_widget'  => '</aside>',
        'before_title'  => '<h1 class="widget-title">',
        'after_title'   => '</h1>',
    ) );

    register_sidebar( array(
        'name'          => __( 'Footer Sidebar', 'topcat' ),
        'id'            => 'sidebar-footer',
        'description'   => 'Footer widgets go here',
        'before_widget' => '<aside id="%1$s" class="widget %2$s">',
        'after_widget'  => '</aside>',
        'before_title'  => '<h1 class="widget-title">',
        'after_title'   => '</h1>',
    ) );
}
add_action( 'widgets_init', 'topcat_widgets_init' );
```

As we can see in the previous image, we just need to add a different title, ID, and a description. Now, we can see our new widget area by navigating to **Appearance** | **Widgets**:

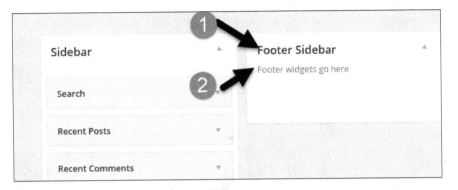

In the preceding image, we can see that our new sidebar, the footer sidebar, has been added beside the old sidebar. Underneath it, our new description **Footer widgets go here** has been added, too.

 We have to click on the arrow in the top-right corner for the area to expand so we can see the new description.

In order to see our sidebars on the live website, we have to complete the following two steps:

- Declare the sidebar (usually in `sidebar.php`)
- Call the `dynamic_sidebar()` function in order to display the sidebar in our theme

 More information about the `dynamic_sidebar()` function can be found in *Chapter 10, Submitting Your Theme to WordPress.org* of our book or in it's Codex page at `http://codex.wordpress.org/Function_Reference/dynamic_sidebar`.

Since we are using the underscores theme, the sidebar declaration code is provided in `sidebar.php`:

```php
if ( ! is_active_sidebar( 'sidebar-1' ) ) {
    return;
}
?>


<div id="secondary" class="widget-area" role="complementary">
    <?php dynamic_sidebar( 'sidebar-1' ); ?>
</div><!-- #secondary -->
```

As we can see from the preceding screenshot, we are checking whether the sidebar with the ID `sidebar-1` has widgets in it. If it has, the result will return true, and if it doesn't, it will return false. If the result is true, our code will proceed to the next section where the sidebar will be loaded with `dynamic_sidebar( 'sidebar-1' );`. Since we currently have a number of widgets loaded in the default sidebar, if we go to **Appearance | Widgets**, we will see the following:

These widgets are also loaded on our home page in the same order:

HOME BLOG FRONT PAGE SAMPLE PAGE ABOUT THE TESTS LEVEL 1 LOREM IPSUM

PAGE 2 PAGE 3

TEMPLATE: STICKY

January 7, 2013 | | Uncategorized | Edit

This is a sticky post.

There are a few things to verify:

- The sticky post should be distinctly recognizable in some way in comparison to normal posts. You can style the title, sticky class (.sticky) if you are using the post_class() function to generate your post classes, which is a best practice.
- They should show above all the very top of the blog index page, even though they could be several posts back chronologically.
- They should still show up again in their chronologically correct postion in time, but without the sticky indicator.
- If you have a plugin or widget that lists popular posts or comments, make sure that this sticky post is not always at the top of those lists unless it really is popular.

Tags: % sticky % template

Leave a comment

HELLO WORLD!

October 15, 2014 | | Uncategorized | Edit

Welcome to WordPress. This is your first post. Edit or delete it, then start blogging!

Tags:

1 Comment

MARKUP: HTML TAGS AND FORMATTING

January 11, 2013 | | Markup | Edit

Headings

Header one

Header two

Header three

Header four

Header five

Header six

Blockquotes

Single line blockquote:

> Stay hungry. Stay foolish.

Multi line blockquote with a cite reference:

> People think focus means saying yes to the thing you've got to focus on. But that's not what it means at all. It means saying no to the hundred other good ideas that there are. You have to pick carefully. I'm actually as proud of the things we haven't done as the things I have done. Innovation is saying no to 1,000 things.
>
> — Steve Jobs – Apple Worldwide Developers' Conference, 1997

Tables

Employee	Salary	
John Doe	$1	Because that's all Steve Jobs needed for a salary.
Jane Doe	$100K	For all the blogging she does.
Fred Bloggs	$100M	Pictures are worth a thousand words, right? So Jane x 1,000.
Jane Bloggs	$100B	With hair like that?! Enough said...

Definition Lists

Definition List Title
  Definition list division.

Startup
  A startup company or startup is a company or temporary organization designed to search for a repeatable and scalable business model.

#dowork
  Coined by Rob Dyrdek and his personal body guard Christopher "Big Black" Boykins, "Do Work" works as a self motivator, to motivating your friends.

Do It Live
  I'll let Bill O'Reilly will explain this one.

Unordered Lists (Nested)

- List item one
  - List item one
    - List item one
    - List item two
    - List item three
    - List item four
  - List item two
  - List item three
  - List item four
- List item two
- List item three
- List item four

Ordered List (Nested)

1. List item one
   1. List item one
      1. List item one
      2. List item two
      3. List item three
      4. List item four
   2. List item two
   3. List item three
   4. List item four
2. List item two
3. List item three
4. List item four

HTML Tags

Recent Posts

- Hello world!
- Markup: HTML Tags and Formatting
- Markup: Image Alignment
- Markup: Text Alignment
- Markup: Title With Special Characters

Recent Comments

- Mr WordPress on Hello world!
- John Doe on Edgar Ceron Ips Content
- Jane Doe on Protected: Template: Password Protected (the password is "enter")
- Jane Doe on Template: Comments
- John Doe on Template: Comments

Archives

- October 2014
- January 2013
- March 2012
- January 2012
- March 2011
- October 2010
- September 2010
- August 2010
- July 2010
- June 2010
- May 2010
- April 2010
- March 2010
- February 2010
- January 2010
- October 2009
- September 2009
- August 2009
- July 2009
- June 2009
- May 2009

Categories

- aciform
- antiquarian
- arrangement
- asphalt
- Auriter
- Cat A
- Cat B
- Cat C
- chardonnette
- classiculae
- Child 1
- Child 2
- Child Category 01
- Child Category 02
- Child Category 03
- Child Category 04
- Child Category 05
- clambake
- digitalisation
- disinfection
- dissheds
- enhancer
- Edgar Ceron
- emphasis
- graduate01
- felicific
- Foo A
- Foo B
- Foo Parent
- green banish
- Grandchild Category
- libero mauris
- lindividualisation
- jumbler
- Markup
- litoris
- monovalation
- multitionat
- nailer
- nonfinancamer
- Parent
- Parent Category
- preisematice
- Post Formats
- prevaricaturh
- bedbell
- quatriezr
- vania scilica
- nutitusin ittmel
- thaucitban
- clout
- full
- indisciplina
- limbian
- Template
- Uncategorized
- Unpublished
- userhhaeriind
- upon
- untitised
- untilindividual
- chelation
- users

Meta

- Site Admin
- Log out
- Entries RSS
- Comments RSS
- WordPress.org

December 2014

S	M	T	W	T	F	S
	1	2	3	4	5	6
7	8	9	10	11	12	13
14	15	16	17	18	19	20
21	22	23	24	25	26	27
28	29	30	31			

« Oct

Why do we see this sidebar? We see it because it was called in the `index.php`, `page.php`, `search.php`, and `single.php` archive templates with the `get_sidebar();` function call.

> In order to make everything clear, we need to include the `sidebar.php` file with the `get_sidebar()` function. On the other side, the `dynamic_sidebar()` function is actually responsible for displaying the sidebar.

In our case, we are going to use one more sidebar in the footer, `sidebar-footer`. We need to save the `sidebar.php` copy as a new file with the name `sidebar-footer.php`, which we are going to edit for our sidebar footer purpose. Here is the look of our `sidebar-footer.php` file:

```
<!-- Custom sidebar code begin -->
    <?php
    if ( ! is_active_sidebar( 'sidebar-footer' ) ) {
        return;
    }
    ?>

<div id="secondary" class="widget-area" role="complementary">
    <?php dynamic_sidebar( 'sidebar-footer' ); ?>
</div><!-- #secondary -->
<!-- Custom sidebar code end -->
```

> Note that we have changed the values from `sidebar-1` to `sidebar-footer`.

In order to see this file in the footer, we need to make the call with `get_sidebar('footer');`.

> Note the `'footer'` name. If we call our footer sidebar file, namely `sidebar-dejan.php`, then our call should be `get_sidebar(dejan');`. Isn't that awesome?

But wait! We still can't see any changes. Do you know why?

It is because we need to go to **Apperance | Widgets** first, and add at least one widget to the archives with a title, in our case `Archives footer`, as you can see it in the next screenshot:

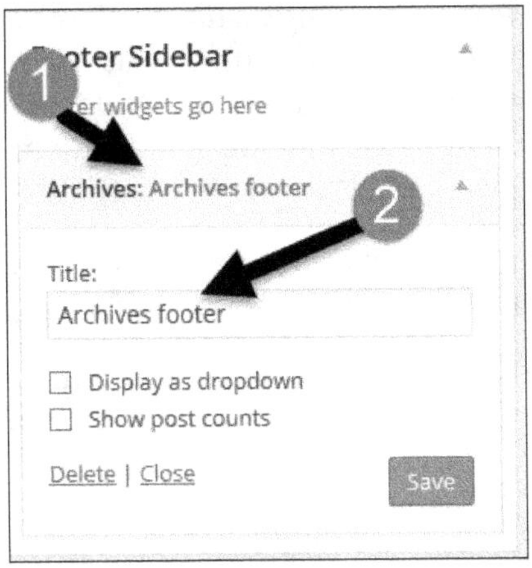

Now, if we scroll to the bottom of our index page or just go to any single post, we will be able to see our archives footer widget, as shown in the following picture:

Styling sidebars

Now that we have created new widget area and are able to add widgets, we should go and style the sidebars. To do this, we need to use the monster widget that we installed in *Chapter 1, Responsive Web Design with WordPress*. The monster widget contains all the default widgets that come with WordPress. It is a great addition to our toolbox as with this, we don't need to load the widgets one by one. When we load the widgets, we style them with our code in order to make sure that our theme is 100 percent compatible with them. What does "compatible" mean?

It means that if the end user puts any or multiple widgets in our sidebar, they should not break the layout of the page nor the widgets' own the layout.

Before we start making big changes, we need to differentiate the right sidebar from the content, and we can do this by simply adding this line to `.widget-area` in `content-sidebar.css`:

```
background: none repeat scroll 0 0#f8f8f8;
```

Here is the new look of the right sidebar:

As we can see from the preceding screenshot, we have a dark silver line, which is our background color, on the right. Then, we have our sidebar in light silver color, followed by our content in white.

If we go to our code in the functions.php file, where we defined the sidebar area, we will see the following:

```
register_sidebar( array(
    'name'          => __( 'Sidebar', 'topcat' ),
    'id'            => 'sidebar-1',
    'description'   => '',
    'before_widget' => '<aside id="%1$s" class="widget %2$s">',
    'after_widget'  => '</aside>',
    'before_title'  => '<h1 class="widget-title">',
    'after_title'   => '</h1>',
) );
```

As we can see, our widgets will be contained in <aside id="%1$s" class="widget %2$s"> with the classname named widget. As I don't like the current padding for this class, we will add padding: 30px 10px. The widget class is located in the widgets area in styless.css.

Here is the look we had before the change:

Here is the new look, after the change:

Widget title fonts are too big, so we will add this style to style.css:

```
.widget-title
{
    font-size: 1.7em;
}
```

We also need to differentiate widget's title from the content, and we will do this by adding the ensuing code to the `widget-title` class:

```
border-bottom: 1px dashed #666;
margin: 10px 0px;
```

Now we can scroll down through the page to see the changes. The only things that don't look particularly interesting are the links and unstyled lists:

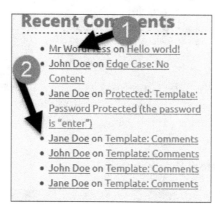

 I have first tried to color our links in blue (#0480b5), but they didn't look appealing as our title is of the same color, meaning there was too much of blue everywhere. I have tested numerous colors (and you should do the same too).

Finally, I came up with this solution that will work best for our links:

```
.widget a,
.widget a:visited,
.widget a:hover
.widget a:active,
#today
{
    color: #666;
    line-height: 1.6;
    text-decoration: none;
    font-weight: 500;
}

.widget a:hover{
    text-decoration: underline;
}
```

Here, we have set all the links in silver color and with a proper line height. After this, we made sure that all the links, except hover links, are not decorated, as shown in the following image:

Finally, we put a font weight of 500 to distinguish links from normal fonts (for example, in the calendar widget.)

> In the calendar widget, we have a special ID for the current day (#today), which I have used to style that number too.

Calendar

December 2014

S	M	T	W	T	F	S
	1	2	3	4	5	6
7	8	9	10	11	12	13
14	15	16	17	18	19	20
21	22	23	24	25	26	27
28	29	30	31			

« Oct

Now, let's add those styles in order to edit lists:

```
.widget ul, .widget li{
    list-style: none;
    margin: 0.3em 0 0;
}
.widget li li { margin-left:1em; }
```

As we can see in the preceding code, we have disabled the width of list styles and then added a margin top of 0.3em. Finally, we added margin-left of 1em for child lists.

Let's see the look of lists that have children:

Pages

Blog

Front Page

Sample Page

About The Tests

  Page Image Alignment

  Page Markup And Formatting

  Clearing Floats

  Page with comments

  Page with comments disabled

Level 1

  Level 2

    Level 3

    Level 3a

    Level 3b

  Level 2a

  Level 2b

Lorem Ipsum

Editing the footer

Our next step is to edit the footer.

First, we need to make our footer distinctive, and we can do this by changing the background color of the .site-footer class in the content-sidebar.php file:

```
background: none repeat scroll 0 0 #2f3336;
```

Now, we are going to create a footer section in the `style.css` file. Since we have just changed the background color of the footer, we need to change the widget title too:

```css
.site-footer .widget-title
{
    font-size: 1.7em;
    border-bottom: 1px dashed #ccc;
    margin: 10px 0px;
    color: #fff;
}
```

Here, we have changed the title color to white and the bottom border color to silver:

Some links and content are almost unreadable, as can be seen in the following image:

We can solve this problem with the following code:

```css
.site-footer .widget a,
.site-footer .widget a:visited,
.site-footer .widget a:hover
.site-footer .widget a:active,
#today
{
    color: #999;
    line-height: 1.6;
    text-decoration: none;
    font-weight: 500;
}
```

With the preceding code, we are making all the widget links in the footer to be of a medium dark silver color:

Now it's more readable, but we still need to fix some parts, right? That number in the brackets is almost invisible:

```
.site-footer .widget ul li
{
    color: #666;
}
```

The preceding code solves the problem as with it, we have added a darker shade of silver so we could distinguish the link from the number.

We fixed the visibility issue for a number of widgets, but the calendar widget is still unfinished:

This line of code will solve the problem for all the unfinished widgets:

```
.site-footer p, .site-footer strong, .site-footer td, .site-footer th,
.site-footer caption
{
    color: #999;
}
```

Now let's have a look at the result:

The only missing part is styling for the current day, and we can solve this with the following line of code:

```
.site-footer #today{
    color: #fff;
    font-weight: 600;
}
```

Here is the look after our change:

Now, as our footer and widgets look fine, we should have them rendered side by side for a desktop look instead of having them one above another:

In order to do this, we just need to add this code:

```
.site-footer .widget {
    float: left;
    width: 30%;
    margin: 0 1rem 2rem 2rem;
}
```

In the preceding code, we've first made all the widgets float to the left so they could be rendered one beside the other. After this, we gave the widgets a width of 30 percent so we can have three widgets in one row. Finally, we set the margins to 0, 1rem, 2rem, and 2rem (top, right, bottom, and left).

The final step with widgets is to make them fluid; that is, if we resize the browser right now, for example to the mobile size, the widgets will still be one beside the other instead of one above the other:

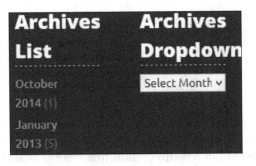

 We have used a percentage width in order to make our layout fluid (part of a responsive layout) but we haven't yet applied the breakpoints. When we apply the breakpoints, the footer will become responsive (it will respond to different sizes of the screen).

In order to make our widgets responsive in the footer, we are going to use the masonry.js library.

Masonry is a great JavaScript grid library that optimizes the layout based on the vertical space size. In our case, it can resize our widgets depending on the layout width. For more information about masonry, visit http://masonry.desandro.com/.

The good thing about masonry is that it already exists in WordPress. We just need to load it in our functions.php file where we are loading all the other .js files:

```
wp_enqueue_script('topcat-masonry','/js/masonry_custom.js',
array('masonry'), false, false);
```

In the preceding code, we have called our custom masonry file where we are going to set the default values for masonry. As we can see from the code, we set masonry as a dependency with array('masonry'). This way, we are loading masonry first and then our custom masonry code.

Now is the time to create the `masonry_custom.js` file in our `themes js` folder.

After this, we should wire the masonry to the footer widgets in our `masonry_custom.js` file with this code:

```
jQuery(document).ready(function($) {
    var $container = $('#sidebar-footer');
    $container.masonry({
        itemSelector: '.widget',
        columnWidth: '.widget',
        isFitWidth: true,
        isAnimated: true

    });
});
```

Here, we have set a container to `#sidebar-footer` and then `itemSelector` to `.widget`, obviously. The interesting part about masonry is that you can set a column width to a CSS class instead of a number, and this change makes it even more responsive. Try both on your own, the number (for example, `300` for `columnWidth`) and CSS class (`.widget` for `columnWidth`), and compare the results.

In the `sidebar-footer` file, we should make sure that our widget container has the `sidebar-footer` ID:

```
<div id="sidebar-footer" class="widget-area" role="complementary">
    <?php dynamic_sidebar( 'sidebar-footer' ); ?>
</div>
```

Finally, when we resize the page, the widgets will load nicely (one beside the other):

However, if we minimize the screen too much, the layout will break.

In order to fix this, we have to customize our masonry custom code in a similar way as we did with `superfish.js`:

```
var phoneSize = 600;
jQuery(document).ready(function($) {

    var $container = $('#sidebar-footer');
    if($(document).width() >= phoneSize) {
        $container.masonry({
            columnWidth: '.widget',
            isFitWidth: true,
            isAnimated: true,
            itemSelector: '.widget'
        });
    }
    $(window).resize(function() {
        if($(document).width() >= phoneSize) {
            $container.masonry({
                columnWidth: '.widget',
                isFitWidth: true,
                isAnimated: true,
                itemSelector: '.widget'
            });

        }
        // < phoneSize disable masonry
        else if($(document).width() < phoneSize) {
            $container.masonry({
```

```
                columnWidth: '.widget',
                isFitWidth: true,
                isAnimated: true,
                itemSelector: '.widget'
            });
            $container.masonry('destroy');
        }
    });
});
```

Here, we have set the phone size variable to 480, which is, actually, the same size as that of content-sidebar.css for a media query. After this, in each section (case), we initialized masonry with its default values. For screen sizes less than the phone size, we disabled masonry and had our widgets displayed one per line. For this, we used the CSS placed in @media screen and (max-width: 480px) in style.css:

```
#sidebar-footer { width: 100%!important; }
    #sidebar-footer .widget {
        width: 100%;
        float: none;
    }
```

When we resize the screen to the phone size, we get only one widget per line:

Working with comments

In this section, we are going to talk about:

- The purpose of comments and why they are important
- Styling comments title
- Styling comments themselves, including the author comments
- Styling comments navigation

The comments feature is a very important part of any website as the comments enable interaction between the site owner and visitors. At the same time, they bring more value to the site, as more information is provided and the site can have more traffic as people who follow or respond to comments can come back. As WordPress has two types of pages, that is, the page and the post (including custom posts), the comments can be displayed on both.

> I recommend that you disable comments on pages of the type "page" on business websites. I don't see the purpose of visitors leaving comments on our "contact us" page or the "about us" page, right?

In order to deal with comments in our theme, we should go to **Template: Comments**, which can be found by using the search widget with the keyword `Template: Comments`, or in `wpadmin` by going to the posts section, searching for the same keyword, and then choosing the **Preview** option. When we finally go to that post, we will see a lot of comments there. Since we don't need to deal with that many, we can go to **Settings | Discussion | Break comments into pages** and type the number `5`.

> Make sure that this option is checked; then, save the changes.

Now we are able to see the number of comments: the comments title (#1), comments toolbar (#2), and comments themselves (#3):

19 THOUGHTS ON "TEMPLATE: COMMENTS"

← *Older Comments*

John Doe says:
March 14, 2013 at 7:57 am Edit
Comment Depth 01

Reply

Jane Bloggs says:
March 14, 2013 at 8:01 am Edit
Comment Depth 02

You are probably wondering how the comments are loaded, right?

If we go to `single.php`, we will see the following code around line 19:

```php
<?php
    // If comments are open or we have at least one comment, load up
the comment template
    if ( comments_open() || get_comments_number() ) :
      comments_template();
    endif;
?>
```

As we can see, this code is checking whether comments are enabled and if there are any comments. If the answer is yes to both, we call the `comment_template()` function, which loads the `comments.php` file. Since `comments.php` has a lot of code, I have created a copy of it called `comments_old.php`.

 We are going to make a number of changes to the `comments.php` file, and in order to avoid the confusion, I will use line numbers as references.

Styling comments title

Before we do anything else, we should change the words around line 28, from `thought` to `comment` and from `thoughts` to `comments`:

This is the code before the change:

```
printf( _nx( 'One thought on &ldquo;%2$s&rdquo;', '%1$s thoughts on
&ldquo;%2$s&rdquo;', get_comments_number(), 'comments title', 'topcat'
),
    number_format_i18n( get_comments_number() ), '<span>' . get_the_
title() . '</span>' );
```

This is the code after the change:

```
printf( _nx( 'One comment on &ldquo;%2$s&rdquo;', '%1$s comments on
&ldquo;%2$s&rdquo;', get_comments_number(), 'comments title', 'topcat'
),
    number_format_i18n( get_comments_number() ), '<span>' . get_the_
title() . '</span>' );;);
```

As you can see now, in the code between lines 33 through 39 and again between 50 through 56, we have a comments header. We really don't need both, so let's delete the one on lines 33 through 39. Since we have deleted the first comments header, we now have this code:

```
<ol class="comment-list">
  <?php
    wp_list_comments( array(
      'style'      => 'ol',
      'short_ping' => true,
    ) );
  ?>
</ol><!-- .comment-list -->
```

In the preceding code, we have the `comment list` class and then the function call to `wp_list_comments()`, which actually displays the comments.

Styling comments

Now, let's change the styling of our comments. In `styles.css`, comments are located in the comments section:

As we can see in the preceding image, we have to do a lot of changes in order to make this look nice.

At first, we will fix the look of links by making them black and underlining them only when they are hovered over:

```
.comment-body a,
.comment-body a:visited,
.comment-body a:active
{
    text-decoration: none;
    color: #000;
}


.comment-body a:hover
{
    text-decoration: underline;
    color: #000;
}
```

Secondly, we should have some space between the image and the author's name, the author's name and the word "says", and the timestamp and the word "edit":

```
.comment-author .fn, .comment-metadata .edit-link
{
    margin: 0.5em;
}
```

After this, let's make the button links (edit and reply) look a little bit different than the other text by making them bold:

```
.comment-metadata .edit-link, .reply{
    font-weight: 600;
}
```

Then, we make the comment's content text italic:

```
.comment-content{
    font-style: italic;
}
```

Finally, we make comments distinctive from `border-bottom`:

```
.comment-list article{
    border-bottom: 1px dashed #666;
}
```

Here is our improved look:

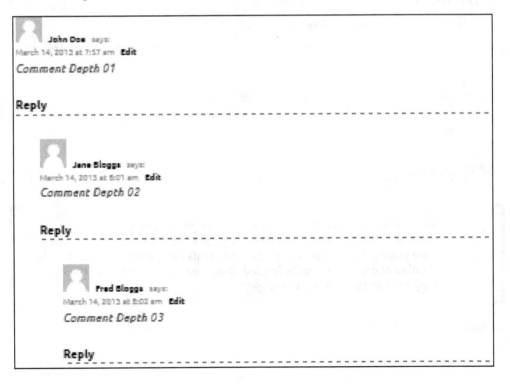

It looks a lot better than it did in the previous image, right? But, if we resize the browser to the mobile size, the list in which comments are located will get more and more nested (indented). To resolve the problem with indentation, add the following code to the media query we used for the sidebar code, which is located at the end of `styles.css`:

```
/* comentscomments */
#comments ol.children {
    list-style-type: none;
    margin-left: 0;
    padding: 0;
}

ul, ol {
    margin: 0 0 1.5em 0em;
}
```

Comments navigation

The final step is to style the comments navigation:

John Doe says:
March 14, 2013 at 11:23 am

We are totally going to blog about these tests!

Reply

← *Older Comments*   *Newer Comments →*

We can have a number of comments on our page/post if, for example, our content is popular. This will make our page too big and it will take a long time to load. To fix this, we can use comments navigation, as with this, the number of comments can be limited; if our readers want to read them all, they can use the comments navigation.

At first, we should take out the word "comments" from the code in `functions.php` around the lines 45 and 46:

```
<div class="nav-previous"><?php previous_comments_link( __( "". "<i
class='fa fa-arrow-left fa-2'></i>  Older ", 'topcat' ) ); ?></
div>
<div class="nav-next"><?php next_comments_link( __( "Newer  <i
class='fa fa-arrow-right fa-2'></i>".  "", 'topcat' ) ); ?></div>
```

In order to make the look more informed, we should also add font awesome arrows (`fa-arrow-left` and `fa-arrow-right`). As comments are less important for us than the content, we should resize font awesome icons with the `.fa-2` class. Let's analyze the CSS code in `style.css`:

```
comment-navigation
.comment-navigation,
.comment-navigation a,
.comment-navigation a:visited,
.comment-navigation a:active
{
    color: #666;
    font-family: "Open Sans",sans-serif;

font-size: 20px;
font-size: 2.0rem !important;
    ;
    line-height: 20;;
    text-transform: uppercase;
    font-weight: 800;
    padding: 10px;
    font-style: normal;
    text-decoration: none;
}
```

In the preceding code, we colored links in the navigation with a darker silver color with `text- decoration` set to `none` (meaning links are not underlined) and `font-size` set to `20px`.

```
.comment-navigation a:hover,.comment-navigation a:hover .fa-arrow-
left, .comment-navigation  a:hover .fa-arrow-right
{
    font-style:normal;
    color: #000;
}
```

Here, we have made the links black when hovered over, and with `font-style:normal;`, we have made sure that when hovered over, fonts will not be in italic.

```
.fa-3
{
    font-size: 20px !important;
     font-size: 2.0rem !important;
 ;
}
```

Here, we made sure that font awesome icons are smaller in comment navigation than in the content part.

Here, we will color font awesome icons to black:

```
.comment-navigation .fa-arrow-left,.comment-navigation .fa-arrow-right
{
    color: #666;
}
```

Let's see the final look of a single comment and the comment navigation under it:

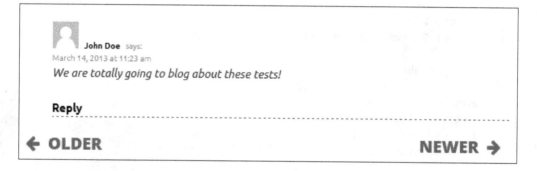

Summary

In this chapter, we learned a lot of useful tips and tricks. In the first section, we learned more about widgets, how to style them, and how to make them responsive. Then, we learned more about sidebars, and finally, we learned how to edit the footer. In the second section, we learned more about comments and how to edit and style them.

I bet you think that you know it all by now, right?

Well, the bad news is that there are a lot of things that we still have to learn; however, the good news is that you are halfway done already!

Go get your coffee and continue on reading, as in the next chapter, we will dive into the wonderful world of images and videos!

In the next chapter, we will learn how to deal with featured images and how to set up and resize these images, image captions, and image galleries. We'll also learn how to make the image galleries responsive.

7
Working with Images and Videos

In this chapter, we will start with something fun and explore, some might say, the most important visual item to look for when designing a website. As we are visual creatures, images and videos are crucial items that we can have on our website in order to attract viewers. This is something that we all want to do, right? Also, YouTube and similar sites have gained a lot of popularity and some people say that YouTube is even more visited than Google's search page. As videos are interactive in some way, they can really boost the viewing of your website, too!

Let's look into everything that we will cover in this chapter:

- Featured images
- How to set up and resize featured images
- Image captions
- Image galleries
- How to make image galleries responsive
- Videos

Featured images

Featured images are images that should represent a post or page on the side of the content. They are optional, which means that the post can have the featured image or may not have it. They used to be called **post thumbnails**, but lately, they have been renamed to **featured images**, as that is the more appropriate name.

We can set a featured image by going to a single post editor, **wpadmin**, and choosing the post that we are going to edit. Inside the single post editor, there is the **Featured Image** option on the right side menu at the bottom of the post:

As we have loaded the theme unit test data, we don't have to create the testing page ourselves. We are going to use `Template: Featured Image (Horizontal)`, and the post can be reached at: `http://localhost/topcat/template-featured-image-horizontal/` (if you have the same setup as I have). If you can't find it there, then you should go to **wpadmin | Posts** and search for the post with the name **Template: Featured Image (Horizontal)**. This post already has a feature image set:

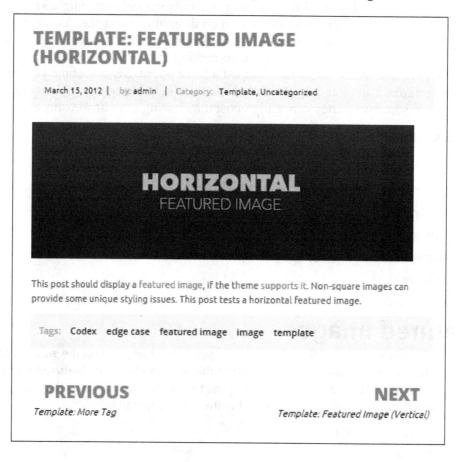

Setting up a featured image

The post mentioned in the preceding screenshot, Template: Featured Image (Horizontal), should also display a featured image, but it doesn't. So, let's analyze the code to see what is going on. If we go to the single.php template, as that's the template for the single post, we will see this line:

```php
<?php get_template_part( 'content', 'single' ); ?>
```

This line means that we are loading a content-single.php template. So, let's open a content-single.php template and look for any code that mentions the post thumbnail. As there is no such code, it means that the featured image functionality is not implemented yet, and we can implement it with just a single line of code:

```php
<?php the_post_thumbnail(); ?>
```

Within the header section, we can find the post thumbnail:

```php
<header class="entry-header">
    <?php the_title( '<h1 class="entry-title">', '</h1>' ); ?>
        <div class="entry-meta">
      <?php  topcat_posted_on(); ?>
    </div><!-- .entry-meta -->
    <?php the_post_thumbnail(); ?>
  </header><!-- .entry-header -->
```

Here is the new look after our changes:

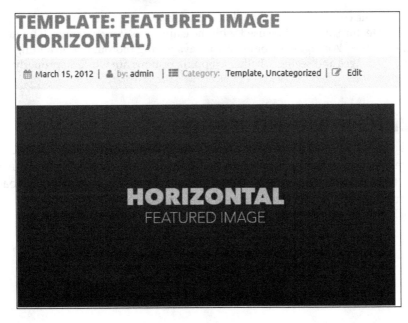

Although WordPress is referring in the content editor as *featured images*, the function name(s) handling the featured images have the names such as `the_post_thumbnail`, meaning that functions with the "old name" era associations are still used.

As our users can now load images of all sizes, we should set sizes that we allow for our featured images. We are going to set this in `functions.php` just below the `add_theme_support( 'post-thumbnails' );` line that we enabled previously:

```
add_theme_support( 'post-thumbnails' );
add_image_size('large-thumbnail', 600, 200, true);
add_image_size('small-thumbnail', 300, 100, true);
```

Here, we are using the `add_image_size` function with which we will set up two thumbnails sizes: 600 x 200 and 300 x 100. The latest parameter that we need to set `true` or `false` is Boolean. The `true` option (the **hard crop** mode) will just cut the image to fill the container that we set, and with the `false` option (soft crop mode), the image will be resized to its proposed value.

More information is available here:

- `http://codex.wordpress.org/Function_Reference/add_image_size`
- `http://www.davidtan.org/wordpress-hard-crop-vs-soft-crop-difference-comparison-example/`

 The cropping option should be used, but as with any important feature, it should be used with the caution, as it may not work for all cases. We highly recommend always testing thoroughly by adding images and seeing whether cropping options are working properly.

Resizing featured images

As we have seen so far, we can set thumbnail sizes for themes in `functions.php`, and that's really a great thing. A problem could arise if our end user loads our theme to their site that already had thumbnails set for their old theme. When they load our theme, thumbnails will look distorted, as they were set for the other theme.

In order to fix this problem, we just have to run the **Regenerate Thumbnails** plugin, which we installed in the *Chapter 1, Responsive Web Design with WordPress*. We go to **wpadmin** | **Tools** | **Regenerate Thumbnails**, press the **Regenerate Thumbnails** button, and we will see the processing screen:

Regenerate Thumbnails

Please be patient while the thumbnails are regenerated. This can take a while if your server is slow (inexpensive hosting) or if you ha
resized. You will be notified via this page when the regenerating is completed.

5%

Abort Resizing Images

Debugging Information

Total Images: 40
Images Resized: 2
Resize Failures: 0

1. "nyto_group" (ID 1710) was successfully resized in 1.523 seconds.
2. "spectacles" (ID 1692) was successfully resized in 1.371 seconds.

Every time we change the theme on any of our sites, we should run this plugin in order to be 100 percent sure that thumbnails in the current theme will be displayed properly.

As we have set the thumbnail sizes, we should implement the change in our `content-single.php` file from: `<?php the_post_thumbnail(); ?>` to this:

```
<?php the_post_thumbnail('large-thumbnail'); ?>
```

As we can see from this code, we added the `'large-thumbnail'` parameter to the function and if we refresh the page now, the image will be resized.

We have set the size for the thumbnail, but we haven't used `small-thumbnail` yet. We will use it in the next chapter, where we will explain index pages.

Finally, if we resize our browser to the mobile size screen, it will look like this:

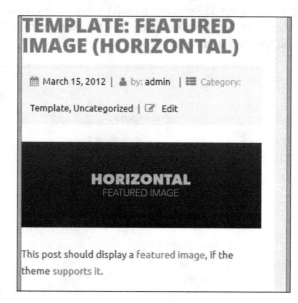

We can see that the image has been resized (the image is responsive), and this is another functionality that was implemented by **underscores**.

That code is located in `style.css` around line 354:

```
img {
    height: auto; /* Make sure images are scaled correctly. */
    max-width: 100%; /* Adhere to container width. */
}
```

If you want to add more properties to this code, feel free to do so.

Image captions

Image captions are used a lot, and their purpose is to provide information about the image. They are optional, but they should be considered for every theme, as some people may use that feature. In order to see the caption, we should use the **Markup: Image Alignment** post. Then, we can scroll down to the example with the image captions:

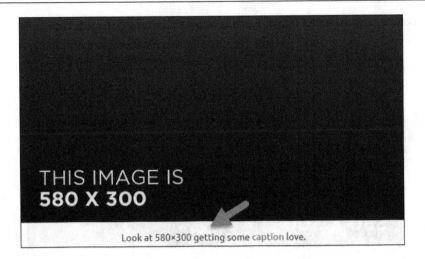

From the preceding screenshot, we can see that the caption below the image looks fine. My advice is to just style it a little bit in order to make it more distinguishable. If we inspect the following code, the image with Firebug, or any other code inspector, we will get this:

```
<figcaption class="wp-caption-text">
Look at 580x300 getting some
<a href="http://en.support.wordpress.com/images/image-settings/"
title="Image Settings">caption</a>
love.
</figcaption>
```

The `wp-caption-text` item is the CSS class that we are looking for and it is located in `style.css`. So, the code that we are looking to delete is:

```
.wp-caption .wp-caption-text {
  margin: 0.8075em 0;
}
```

This code is located somewhere around the line 1,348. The change I suggest we do is to make the text more distinctive by making it italic and adding the same silver background that we used for the sidebar:

```
figcaption {
    padding: 0.8075em 0;
    background: #f8f8f8;
    font-style: italic;
    width: 150px;
    margin: 0;
}
```

Let's see our result now:

There are captions as a part of galleries too. We will cover this in our next section, *Image galleries*.

Image galleries

Image galleries are a great option to share images with end users. We can create the gallery by just going to the single post editor where we want to create the gallery, and simply clicking on the **Add Media** button:

After this, the **Insert Media** menu will show up:

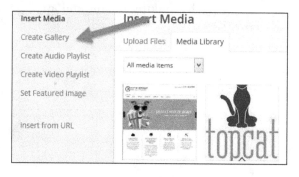

Here, we should click on the **Create Gallery** option. When we click on this option, we will see images loaded on the right-hand side. Then, we just have to click on images that we want to add to the gallery, click on the **Create New Gallery** button at the bottom on the right side, and that's it.

As we have loaded a **Theme Unit Test** data, we don't have to do all this, and we have two posts: **Post Format: Gallery** and **Post Format: Gallery (Tiled).**

Here is the look of the **Post Format: Gallery** post:

As we can see from the preceding screenshot, the captions are taking more space than images. In order to make sure that we are doing everything correctly, we have created a new test gallery, so we can double-check the default size of thumbnails. When we loaded all images, the individual sizes of thumbnails were 150 x 150, which is what we want. we added a CSS to `style.css` in order to get this 150 x 150 size for captions in our existing gallery:

```
.gallery-item  figcaption {
    width: 150px;
}
```

Our result is this:

The caption is of the same width as the image now. After this, we should go to the `12.2 Galleries` section and comment out `text-align: center` in the `.gallery-item` class:

```
.gallery-item {
   display: inline-block;
/*   text-align: center; */
   vertical-align: top;
   width: 100%;
}
```

Now, if we scroll down in the gallery, we will see that some rows don't have enough space between them:

We can solve this problem with just one line of code in `style.css`:

```
figure
{
    margin-bottom: 0.8075em !important;
}
```

Let's view our result now:

Making the gallery responsive

The final step in the creation of a gallery is to make it responsive. For example, if we, resize the browser to the phone size screen, we will get this:

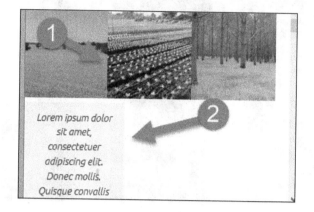

The caption is bigger than its image and images are beside each other, because these images are responsive (they resize together with the screen, so they look good across all devices), and the caption has a fixed size of 150px, as you can see it from our code in style.css:

```
.gallery-item  figcaption {
    width: 150px;
}
```

As the phone screen is too small, we should put our images into their own rows and their captions just below them. Because we are now handling a mobile size screen, we should put our classes in @media screen and (max-width: 480px), which are located in style.css (the same media query that we used for the sidebar and comments):

```
.gallery-item {
        width:100%;
        display: block;
        margin: 2em 1em;
        text-align: center;
    }
```

This code creates our gallery item with width of 100% and centers the item in its row too. If we refresh the browser now, we will see no changes to our div gallery:

```
<div id="gallery-1" class="gallery galleryid-555 gallery-columns-3
gallery-size-thumbnail">
```

This code has a class of `gallery-columns-3`, so we have to make sure that items in this class take `100%` width:

```
.gallery-columns-3 .gallery-item,
    .gallery-columns-4 .gallery-item,
    .gallery-columns-5 .gallery-item,
    .gallery-columns-6 .gallery-item,
    .gallery-columns-7 .gallery-item,
    .gallery-columns-8 .gallery-item,
    .gallery-columns-9 .gallery-item
    {
        max-width: 100%;
    }
```

If we go back to the `gallery` section of our `style.css` file, we will see that we have cases there for `gallery-columns-3` up to `gallery-columns-9`, and the preceding code has covered it all. If we refresh our page in the mobile size view, we will see our images centered, but our captions left-aligned:

Golden Gate Bridge

Let's make our captions take `100%` width and align them to the center too:

```
.gallery-item  figcaption {
            width: 100%;
            text-align: center;
        }
```

Here is our final look:

Bell on wharf in San Francisco

Golden Gate Bridge

Working with videos

Working with videos in WordPress is really easy. For the major video sites (YouTube or Vimeo), we can just copy and paste the URL into the post editor and click on **Publish**, and embedded video will appear on our page or post:

Now, try to resize the screen to the mobile size and you will be pleasantly surprised that the video is a responsive, too. Isn't that great?

> The list of supported video sites can be found here:
> `http://codex.wordpress.org/Embeds`.

As we can see from the link, the list of supported video sites is huge. If, in some case, you would like to post a video that is not located on these sites, you will have to create a custom code for it, and that's out of the scope of our book.

> You should be aware that posting videos on these external sites is the *way to go*, as this way, you are using their bandwidth and not yours. As with most hosting companies, even with those that have unlimited packages, the bandwidth is limited (read the fine print).

Summary

In this chapter, at the beginning, we learned more about featured images and how to set up and resize them. Later on, we tackled the image caption and learned how to create the image gallery and make it responsive. Finally, we learned about videos.

In the next chapter, we will get familiar with template files.

8
Working with Template Files

Template files are very important files for WordPress themes. We have mentioned this previously, but let's repeat it again. In order to have a theme in WordPress, we need to have at least the following files:

- `style.css`
- `functions.php`
- `index.php`

In `style.css`, we define the theme name, a description, and the core CSS for the theme. In the `functions.php` file, we define our own custom functions and calling our styles and JavaScript, and also wireing our theme code to the WordPress core. In the `index.php` file, we display the list of our posts, pages, or any other objects that are listed in that index page. There can be a lot of index pages in our template.

Without further ado, in this chapter we will:

- Learn the template hierarchy of archive pages
- Learn more about excerpts
- Learn how to customize the paging navigation
- Learn how to style sticky posts
- Modify `archive.php`
- Modify `404.php`
- Modify `search.php`

The WordPress template hierarchy

So, let's analyze the WordPress template hierarchy again:

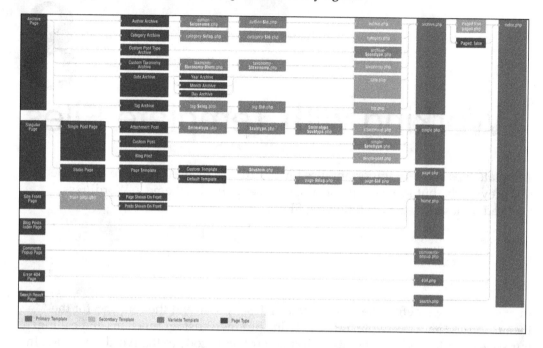

This is taken from: `http://codex.wordpress.org/Template_Hierarchy`. If we start from right to left, we have the `index.php` page, and that page catches all requests that are not explicitly handled by another template. If we want to have a special template for archives, then we can create the `archive.php` (available with our theme) template. For search results, we can use `search.php` (available with our theme). For a missing page/post, we can use `404.php` (available with our theme). So, if we examine the preceding screenshot, we can see that `archive.php` is a child of `index.php`, and `search.php` and `404.php` are children of `index.php`. If we open any of these pages, we will see that they have a similar structure (as they are bootstrap pages too). They just have some code that is unique, as it has to be like that in order to serve the purpose of a page. If we want to see this relationship explained in real life, we can add the `testing archive page` text in the `archive.php` page just under `get_header();`:

```
get_header(); ?>
testing archive page
```

From the previous explanation, we know that the archive.php page is an index page for archives, but if we check the preceding screenshot, we will see that it's a parent page for author.php, category.php and tag.php. As we don't have any of these available, archive.php can and will be used as a template for these situations. If we go to the index page of our website, we will see the first post with the Template: Sticky name . This post has tags at the bottom, and if we click on any of the tags, we will see this:

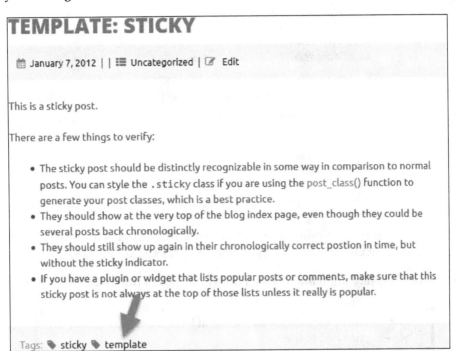

We should go to the index page for this tag (template):

As we can see from the preceding screenshot, our URL (**#1**) says it's a tag page for the `template` tag: `http://localhost/topcat/tag/template/`.

Secondly, the **template** tag name is listed above the post's title (**#2**).

> This page will list all posts that have the `template` tag attached to them.

Finally, the `testing archive page` text that we have added to `archive.php` is shown here (**#3**), which means that `archive.php` was used to that purpose. The same thing will happen if we click on any category. We will go to the index page of the category for which our `archive.php` page is used, and we will see the same text that we added to the archive page.

Excerpts

As we have a lot of posts loaded with our test data and hopefully, our customers will have a lot of posts too, displaying the full content on index pages is not appropriate as it takes too much space. If somebody is looking for something, it's really confusing, and it takes valuable time. This is where the excerpt functionality comes to the rescue.

Excerpts can be customized but, by default, they display the first 55 words of the article and ends with [...], which is called a **hellip** or an **ellipsis** symbol.

More info is available at `http://codex.wordpress.org/Function_Reference/the_excerpt`.

As we have mentioned previously, our `index.php` file is a bootstrap file with calls to other files that provide page sections. The `get_template_part( 'content', get_post_format() );` line includes the `content-[post_type].php` file, and if that file doesn't exist, it includes the `content.php` file, which provides the content. In our case, it includes `content.php`. Suppose that we go to `content.php` and comment out this code:

```
the_content( sprintf(
            __( 'Continue reading %s <span class="meta-nav">&rarr;</
span>', 'topcat' ),
            the_title( '<span class="screen-reader-text">"', '"</
span>', false )
            ) );
```

And just leave the excerpt part:

```
the_excerpt().
```

Here is the full code example where we have commented out the _content() part:

```
<?php
    /* translators: %s: Name of current post */

        /*
    the_content( sprintf(
        __( 'Continue reading %s <span class="meta-nav">&rarr;</span>',
'topcat' ),
        the_title( '<span class="screen-reader-text">"', '"</span>',
false )
    ) );
        */
    the_excerpt();

?>
```

We will have our excerpt displayed on our index page, as you can see on the following image:

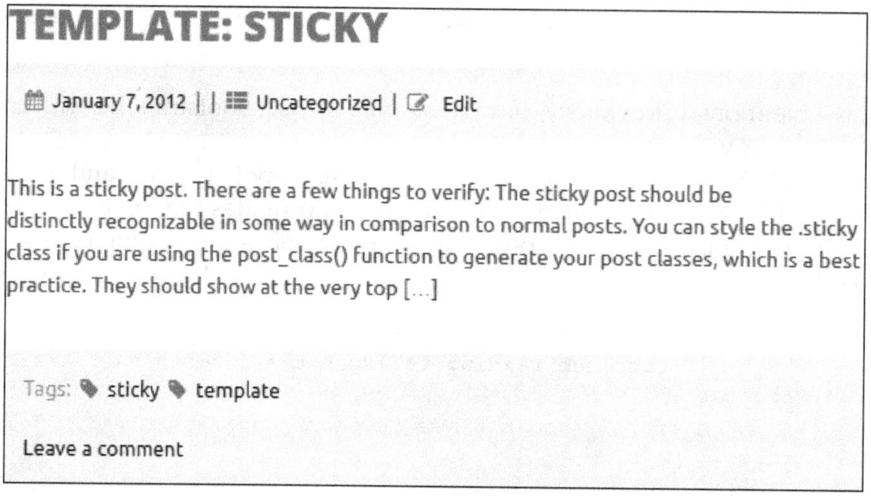

Isn't this easy? The only part missing here is the **Read More** button (link). We also have a footer there with tags and option to leave the comment, and this is really not needed on the index page, so we will take the footer out:

```php
<?php topcat_entry_footer(); ?>
```

Replace this line (in `content.php`) with the **Read More** link:

```php
<?php echo '<a href="' . get_permalink() . '" title="' . __('Read More ', 'topcat') . get_the_title() . '" >Read More  <i class="fa fa-arrow-circle-o-right"></i></a>'; ?>
```

As you can see, we have added the awesome icon font to the code:

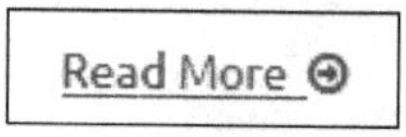

Now, we just have to style the link properly, and that's it. We will do this in the `Posts and pages` section (10.1) of `style.css`.

At the end of the section, we should put this code:

```css
.entry-footer,
.entry-footer a,
.entry-footer a:visited,
.entry-footer a:active
{
```

```
    color: #000;
    font-weight: 600;
    font-family: "Open Sans",sans-serif;
    text-decoration: none;
}

.entry-footer a:hover
{
    color: #0480b5;
    font-family: "Open Sans",sans-serif;
    text-decoration: underline;
}
```

The first part is to make the links black and bold in order to make them more distinctive from the content text, make them undecorated (meaning no underline), and assign them a font family. On hovering, we color the text with blue and give it an underline decoration.

Featured images

The next step is to put featured images in the content template, and all it takes is adding one line:

```
<header class="entry-header">
    <?php the_title( sprintf( '<h1 class="entry-title"><a href="%s"
rel="bookmark">', esc_url( get_permalink() ) ), '</a></h1>' ); ?>

    <?php if ( 'post' == get_post_type() ) : ?>
    <div class="entry-meta">
      <?php topcat_posted_on(); ?>
    </div><!-- .entry-meta -->
        <?php the_post_thumbnail('small-thumbnail'); ?>
    <?php endif; ?>
</header><!-- .entry-header -->
```

Post thumbnails or featured images

While listing the excerpts of posts, we want to also show their post thumbnail—if they are available. This is why featured images are also called post thumbnails—like thumbnails in a gallery, they represent the post in the list context.

If you remember, we have added the two sizes of post thumbnails in the *Chapter 6, Responsive Widgets, Footer, and Comments*, and we used only the large one for the single post. For the index page, we are using a small thumbnail:

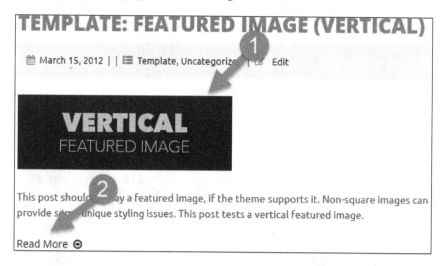

We can see a small thumbnail (**#1**) and the look of the **Read More** link (**#2**) in the preceding screenshot.

Customizing the paging navigation

If we scroll to the end of the index page, we will see the **Older posts** link:

This is part of our current navigation. The good thing with this navigation is that we have it and the bad thing is that is really simple and if we have a lot of posts, this navigation is not that helpful. Paging will be more helpful, as there we will have boxes with page numbers. Then we will be able to skip more pages at the same time instead of just going from one page to another. Our navigation code is contained in the `topcat_paging_nav()` function that is located in the `template-tags.php` file with other custom functions. As we want to use the more sophisticated solution, I have found the code that has a paging functionality (this code is actually used in the Twenty Fourteen theme, that has been tested a lot and because of that it is good).

The updated `template-tags.php` file is provided with the code for this chapter.

Make sure that you change the instances of the word (domain) from `twentyfourteen` to `topcat` in this code.

Here is the example:

```
" 'prev_text' => __( '<i class="fa fa-arrow-left fa-4"></i>
Previous', 'twentyfourteen' ), "
" 'prev_text' => __( '<i class="fa fa-arrow-left fa-4"></i>
Previous', 'topcat' ), "
```

Here is the code section where we have to make changes for the navigation located in `/inc/template-tags.php`:

```
// Set up paginated links.
$links = paginate_links( array(
    'base'      => $pagenum_link,
    'format'    => $format,
    'total'     => $wp_query->max_num_pages,
    'current'   => $paged,
    'mid_size'  => 1,
    'add_args'  => array_map( 'urlencode', $query_args ),
    'prev_text' => __( '<i class="fa fa-arrow-left fa-4"></i>
Previous', 'topcat' ),
    'next_text' => __( 'Next <i class="fa fa-arrow-right fa-4"></i>',
'topcat' ),
) );
```

Here is the current look of the paging navigation:

← Previous 1 2 3 4 Next →

Now, let's start with styling our pagination:

```
.pagination,
.pagination  a,
.pagination  a:visited,
.pagination  a:active
{
    color: #0480b5;
    font-family: "Open Sans",sans-serif;
    font-size: 1.6rem !important;
```

```
        font-size: 16px;
        line-height: 16px;
        text-transform: uppercase;
        font-weight: 800;
        padding: 10px;
        font-style: normal;
        text-decoration: none;
}
```

In the previous code, we are coloring our pagination in blue, we are making fonts to be uppercase and a 1.6rem size, and finally, we are making sure none of the links are underlined. Take a look at this code:

```
.pagination .current
{
    color: #666;
}
```

In the next code, we are coloring hover links to dark silver and we are making sure that on hovering, they will be underlined:

In the following code, we are coloring current page number to dark silver:

```
.pagination a:hover
{
    color: #666;
    font-family: "Open Sans",sans-serif;
    font-size: 1.6rem !important;
    font-size: 16px;
    line-height: 16px;
    text-transform: uppercase;
    font-weight: 800;
    padding: 10px;
    font-style: normal;
    text-decoration: underline;
}
```

With this code, we are making sure that our pagination is centered, as it looks better like that:

```
.pagination
{
    text-align:  center;
}
```

The original pagination used HTML special characters for arrows, but as we are using the font awesome for them on other sections, it will be appropriate to use it for this navigation too. In order to use the font awesome fonts, we have to change the code in `template-tags.php`:

```
$links = paginate_links( array(
        'base'      => $pagenum_link,
        'format'    => $format,
        'total'     => $wp_query->max_num_pages,
        'current'   => $paged,
        'mid_size'  => 1,
        'add_args'  => array_map( 'urlencode', $query_args ),
        'prev_text' => __( '<i class="fa fa-arrow-left fa-4"></i>
Previous', 'topcat' ),
        'next_text' => __( 'Next <i class="fa fa-arrow-right fa-4"></
i>', 'twentyfourteen' ),
    ) );
```

Changes are marked in bold in the previous code. After this, we have to make changes in `style.css`. As we want these arrows to be smaller than the arrows in other sections, we will use `.fa-4` (font awesome 4 class), and because the fonts are the size of `16px`, we should have the font awesome icons to have a `16px` size, too:

```
.fa-4{
font-size: 16px;
font-size: 1.6rem !important;
    }
```

Also, we want icons to change color on the hover to our dark silver color. To achieve this, we will use the following code:

```
.pagination a:hover .fa-arrow-right,
.pagination a:hover .fa-arrow-left
{
    color: #666;
}
```

Styling sticky posts

Sticky post is the most important post that we want to show at the top of all posts, even before the latest posts. As we have mentioned previously, we can check whether our post is sticky; if we go to the post editor and at the top-right **Publish** section, it will display this:

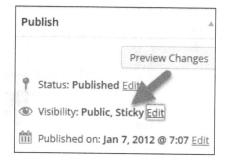

If it's not a sticky post and we want to make it sticky, we should just click on the **Edit** button and check the **Stick this post to the front page** option:

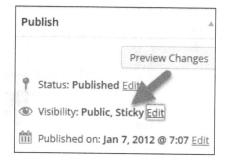

If the post is a sticky, WordPress adds a `sticky` class to the markup:

```
<article class="post-1241 post type-post status-publish
format-standard sticky hentry category-uncategorized
tag-sticky-2 tag-template" id="post-1241">
```

> By default, WordPress adds a `sticky` class to the markup only under certain circumstances on index pages but not on single post pages.

Then, we just have to find the sticky class in our `style.css` file and add the border and padding:

```css
.sticky {
    display: block;
    border: 1px dashed #666;
    padding: 10px;
}
```

Let's see our result:

TEMPLATE: STICKY

📅 January 7, 2012 | | ☷ Uncategorized | ✐ Edit

This is a sticky post. There are a few things to verify: The sticky post should be distinctly recognizable in some way in comparison to normal posts. You can style the .sticky class if you are using the post_class() function to generate your post classes, which is a best practice. They should show at the very top [...]

Read More ⊕

Modifying archive.php

As we have mentioned at the beginning of this chapter, while analyzing the first image (the template hierarchy), the `archive.php` template is the parent template for archives for authors, categories, post types, taxonomies, dates, and tags. Overall, it displays the array of posts that match the specific post type (mentioned previously).

We have tested this functionality by clicking on a category or a tag in our index page, and we got the output from `archive.php`. Take a look at the code in `archive.php`:

```php
if ( is_category() ) :
    single_cat_title();
elseif ( is_tag() ) :
    single_tag_title();
elseif ( is_author() ) :
    printf( __( 'Author: %s', 'topcat' ), '<span class="vcard">' . get_the_author() . '</span>' );
```

We will see that the output is just a basic one. For example, if the end user clicks on the **Template** category, he/she will get this output:

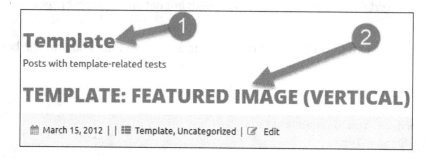

The category name (**Template**) will be displayed above the title, but it doesn't say anywhere whether that's a category, a tag, or something else. By adding just one line of the code, we will make it more explicit:

```
echo( __( 'Category: ', 'topcat' ) );
single_cat_title();
```

We can make the same change with tags:

```
echo( __( 'Tag: ', 'topcat' ) );
single_tag_title();
```

The only thing that we should change is the color of that title, as it's currently the same color as the post title and it's hard to differentiate them. We can perform this change by adding an `archive-title` class to this line:

```
<h1 class="page-title archive-title">
```

With just adding the `archive-title` class to our `style.css` file:

```
.archive-title{
    color: #666;
}
```

We should add this code to 10.1 sections: **Posts and pages**. Our final result is:

We will get the same look if we click on any tags instead of categories, as `archive.php` is a fallback template.

Modifying 404.php

`404.php` is the page that shows the warning message when end user tries to go to a page that doesn't exists, for example: `http://localhost/topcat/page1234` as you can see in the following image:

Here, we first search for the term (# **1**), and then we get the message (# **2**). Below the message, we get the search box (# **3**)—same one as in `search.php`—so we can search for something that exists in the system, as maybe, we have misspelled the page. Below that, we see some other widgets (# **4**)—**Recent Posts**, **Most Used Categories**, and so on—that will give us more options to find the stuff that we are looking for. So, at first, we should change the color of the title by adding an `archive-title` class to this line:

```
<h1 class="page-title archive-title"><?php _e( 'Oops! That page
can&rsquo;t be found.', 'topcat' ); ?></h1>
```

As we don't have the sidebar on this page and it can be helpful to end user, we should add it to our `search.php` page just before the call for the footer:

```php
<?php get_sidebar(); ?>
<?php get_footer(); ?>
```

Let's see how our page looks like after the changes:

It looks pretty good, right?

Modifying search.php

The `search.php` file is in the same level as `archive.php` and its purpose is to show the results of the search, and if there are no results, it should show the message. As we already did a lot of customization, we just need to do the basic styling and test the search. At this moment, we don't have a search form, but we can test the search by adding parameters to the URL, for example:

```
http://localhost/topcat/?s=test
```

Here, we are adding the `?s=test` parameter, which means that we are searching for any post or page that contains the `test` term. Our result is:

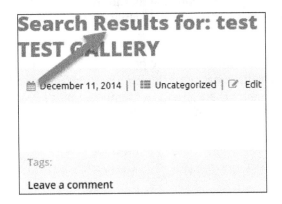

The result looks good, as we have found the matches for our search. The only thing that we should change is the color of the page title; in our case, this is **Search Results for: test**; to distinguish it from the post title, **TEST GALLERY**. In order to do this, we just have to go to `search.php` and add the `archive-title` class to this line:

```
<h1 class="page-title archive-title"><?php printf( __( 'Search
Results for: %s', 'topcat' ), '<span>' . get_search_query() .
'</span>' ); ?></h1>
```

This is the result:

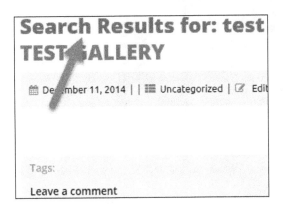

Summary

In this chapter, we have learned about the hierarchy of template files, excerpts, how to customize the paging navigation, how to style sticky posts, `archive.php`, `404.php`, and `search.php`.

In the next chapter, we will work on static pages and their templates and we will learn how to add extra functionality with plugins. We will cover the home page, as its layout has more elements than other pages and it doesn't have a sidebar, which means that we will add another `CSS` file for that case.

9
Working with Static Pages and Adding the Extra Functionality with Plugins

We have left the best for last. With this chapter, we are wrapping the development part of our book.

> *Posts are entries listed in reverse chronological order on the blog home page or on the posts page if you have set one wpadmin-> Settings->Reading. If you have created any sticky posts, those will appear before the other posts. If you are using WordPress as a blogging platform you will be mostly using posts there. You can organize your posts by using categories and tags.*

> *Pages are static and are not listed by date. Pages do not use tags or categories. An About page is the classic example of a static page.*

Static pages are a crucial part of WordPress themes as we are giving our customers premade solutions that they can configure to their needs.

Let's see what we will cover in this chapter:

- Creating and assigning the page template
- Creating alternative styles for the home page
- Setting the `slider` plugin

- Setting the `services` plugin
- Checking whether there are services and how to list them
- Making the home page responsive
- Creating the **Contact Us** page with a `contact us` plugin that is a part of Jetpack

Home page

Home page is the landing page of our website and its purpose is to attract customers and provide the most important information. As home page usually has a different look than other pages, we have to create a custom code in order to match our needs. Here is the look that we want for our home page:

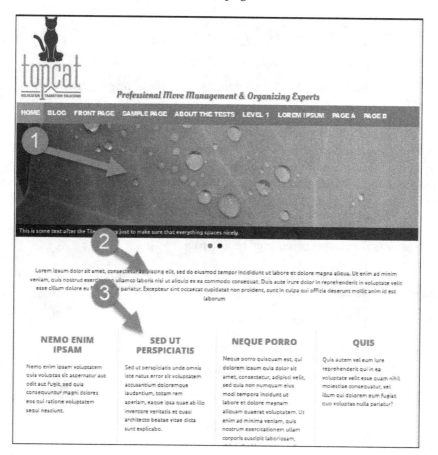

As we can see from the preceding screenshot, we will have three sections there: the slider (**1**), short description (**2**) and the list of services (**3**). All these features are optional, although I advise using them all, as they became a *de-facto* standard for business-oriented templates in the last few years.

> If you want to know more about the features for business templates, check the following sites:
> - `https://wordpress.org/themes/search/business/`
> - `http://themeforest.net/category/wordpress/corporate`
>
> Here, you will see that a majority of themes have the features that I have just mentioned

The home page template

As we have mentioned, we are going to create a custom template that will serve the purpose of the home page. In order to do this we have to go in our editor and create the `front-page.php` file. In this file, we should add the following code, in order to make this file a page template:

```
/*
Template Name: Home Page
*/
```

When we added this code, we got a new option in our page editor. However, before we make any changes, we should go to the page editor by navigating to **wpadmin | Pages | Add New** and create a new page with the Home name. After this, we will be able to see the template dropdown in the **Page Attributes** section on the right, and there, we should choose the **Home Page** template:

That is how we assign the template to the page in editor.

We could assign anything to the template name. We are just using `Template Name: Home Page` for consistency and to make our life easier, as this template name is clearly saying what this template is about.

Now, we should go to **Appearances | Customize** in **wpadmin** and assign a **Home** page as **Static Front Page**:

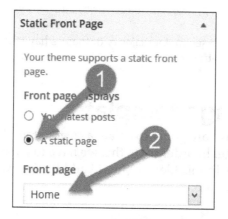

In the previous image, in the step #1, we are choosing a radio option **A static page**, and in step #2, we are choosing our **Home** page from the dropdown. Now, when we click on a home link in our menu or on a logo, we will be taken to our new home page.

Styles for the home template

As we were able to see from the first image at the beginning of this chapter, our home page is going to look different than other pages. It will not have the right sidebar and the content will take 100 percent. Because of all this, we should have a separate CSS file for this purpose.

 As we already have a `content-sidebar.css` file in our `layouts` folder, I recommend that you create a copy of this file. We can reuse a lot of code there and we should name the new file `content.css`.

In order to use content.css on our home page, we have to add this code to our functions.php file:

```
if ( is_page_template( 'front-page.php' ) ) {
    wp_enqueue_style( 'topcat-layout-css',
get_template_directory_uri() . '/layouts/content.css' );
}
else
{
    wp_enqueue_style( 'topcat-layout-css', get_template_directory_
uri() . '/layouts/content-sidebar.css' );
}
```

In the content.css file, we should make some changes. For example, we should change this class:

```
.site-main {
    margin: 0 5% 0 0;
}
```

To the following:

```
.site-main {
    margin: 0;
}
```

We should also delete the .site-content .widget-area class, as we are not going to use the widget area in this template.

Then, in the desktop styles media query:

```
/*desktop styles*/
@media only screen and (min-width:769px) {
```

We should make the content area taking 100% instead of 70%, and delete the float, as we don't need it :

```
.content-area {
        width: 100%;
    }
```

In order to display the content entered in the editor in our home template, we have to add this code to `home-page.php`:

```php
<?php if (have_posts()) : while (have_posts()) : the_post();?>
        <?php the_content(); ?>
    <?php endwhile; endif; ?>
```

Slider plugin

As we want to make our site more interactive, we should install a `slider` plugin. There are a lot of free and premium slider plugins that we could use, but as this is a training book, we will use the free one so that everybody can have the access to it. For this purpose, we will use a Meta Slider, which is currently the most popular free slider plugin on the WordPress.org website.

It can be downloaded from here: `https://wordpress.org/plugins/ml-slider/`.

> For my professional projects, I was using a LayerSlider, which is a premium plugin. You can check it out here: `http://codecanyon. net/item/layerslider-responsive-wordpress-slider- plugin-/1362246`.

The great thing with our Meta Slider plugin is that we can set it up in its own editor, grab a shortcode, paste it in our page, and that's it. Shortcodes are custom features that can be called from the post or page editor; for example, gallery can be called with `[gallery]`. Our Meta Slider will be called with this code: `[metaslider id=1734]`.

Now, let's set up the slider:

Here, we should first add the first slide, and then choose the image (**#1**), general description (**#2**), and URL (**#3**).

 Please note that I didn't choose anything for our URLs at this point.

Then, we should choose which slider we want to use, as Meta Slider has many options. In this case, let's use the first option: Flex slider (**#4**). As our content width is `1000px`, we should choose a width of **1000px** (**#5**), too and a height of **273px** (**#6**).

These sizes work with images that I have used, and I recommend that you use the same images.

These images were provided as a part of the Theme Unit Test Data and we can find them by just choosing the **Add slide** option in **Media Library**, and they should be somewhere on the first page.

After dimensions, we should choose the **Fade** effect (**#7**) and the **Default** theme (**#8**), and we should also select the **Arrows** checkbox (**#9**) and **Dots** for the navigation. Let's look at the advanced settings:

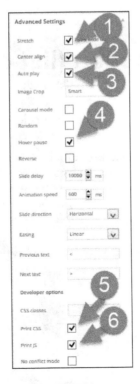

In the advanced settings, we should choose:

- The **Stretch** option (#1)
- **Center align** (#2)
- **Auto play** (#3)
- **Hover pause** (#4)
- **Print CSS** (#5)
- **Print JS** (#6)

For the final step, we should copy the shortcode from the usage section and paste it in the page editor:

Permalink: http://localhost/topcat/   View Page

📷 Add Media   🖼 Add slider   ⊙ Add Slider   Visual   Text (HTML)

b *i* link b-quote del ins img ul ol li code more close tags   ⤢

[metaslider id=1734]

In our case, the code is [metaslider id=1734], and in your case, the code (id number) may be different.

The Services section (list of services)

In this section, we will create the option to list services, and in order to do that, we have to create the option for our users to add services. The best way to do this is to use the plugin, which will add custom post services to our **wpadmin** dashboard.

 Custom posts help end user differentiate one type of post from other as in the database, all posts are saved on the same place. In our example, our user can choose the services option in **wpadmin** and add new services. Later on, when we want to show results, we are going to search for posts of the type service to display.

I have created the plugin that will add custom post type services to **wpadmin,** and this plugin can be downloaded from https://github.com/dejanmarkovic/nyto-services-cpt.

When we download the plugin, we will just have to install and activate it, and then we will see the **Services** option in **wpadmin**:

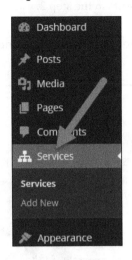

Then, we should go there and add new services, same as we add any other post or page:

In the step 1 (#1), we will press the **Add New** button to add a new service, and in the step 2 (#2), we can see the services that are already added.

> In your case, you will have to add services first in order to see the results in the step 2.

After we add services to our system, we should go and handle the results in our `front-page.php` file:

```php
<?php
/*
Template Name: Home Page
*/

get_header(); ?>
<div id="primary" class="content-area">
    <main id="main" class="site-main" role="main">
        <?php if ( have_posts() ) : while ( have_posts() ) : the_post();?>
            <?php the_content(); ?>
        <?php endwhile; endif; ?>

        <!-- check if nyto-services-cpt plugin is installed (it is required if we are going to use the Services feature) -->
        <?php if ( is_plugin_active( 'nyto-services-cpt/nyto_services_cpt.php' ) ) {
            ?>
            <!-- Display custom posts of type service -->
            <?php $loop = new WP_Query( array( 'post_type' => 'service' ) ); ?>
            <?php
            if ( $loop->found_posts > 0 ) {
                $service_class = '';
                if ( $loop->found_posts <= 4 ) {
                    $service_class = round( 100 / $loop->found_posts );
                }
            ?>
                <!-- begin services row -->
                <section class="inline-block-center services_section">
                    <?php while ( $loop->have_posts() ) : $loop->the_post(); ?>
                        <div class=<?php echo 'perc'. "$service_class"; ?>><!-- begin service column wrapper -->
                            <?php  echo '<h2 class="service-title">' . get_the_title(). '</h2>' ; ?>
                            <span class="entry-content service-content">
                                <?php the_content(); ?>
                            </span>
                        </div> <!-- end services column wrapper -->
                    <?php endwhile; ?>
                </section> <!-- end services row -->
            <?php } //closing if services exists ?>
        <?php } //closing if services exists ?>
    </main>
</div><!-- #primary -->
<?php get_footer(); ?>
```

First (**#1**), we check whether our plugin is installed and activated. If the plugin is not there, we should not display the services. This means that if our end user installs the plugin and adds the services but later on, changes his/her mind and uninstalls the plugin, the services should not be displayed. Next (**#2**), we execute a query first in order to get posts of the type of service; then (**#3**), we check whether there are any services in the database, and if there are, then we will display them; if not, we will not display anything in this section. As you can see, each of the sections is optional, as we have mentioned previously. Later on (**#4**), we define a `$service_class` variable that is going to be used as a CSS helper for our layout.

Next (**#5**), we check whether there are 4 or less services in the database, as this solution is customized for up to four services.

 This code can handle only up to 4 services, and that will be enough for our project.

Later on (**#6**), we are doing a calculation for our service class; if there is only one service in the database, the services section will take 100 percent of that width; if there are 2 services, they will take 50 percent each; if there are 3 services, each service will take 33 percent; if there are 4 services, each service will take 25 percent. For these cases, we are going to use CSS classes' `perc33`, `perc25`, and so on:

```css
/* percentage size of services boxes */
.perc33{
    max-width: 33%;
}
.perc25{
    width: 25%;
}
.perc100{
    width: 100%;
}
.perc50{
    width: 50%;
}
```

This CSS code should go to the `content.css` file's `desktop styles` media query:

```css
/*desktop styles*/
@media only screen and (min-width:769px)
```

Next (**#7**), we add classes which make sure that services will be center-aligned:

```css
/*align services to center */
.inline-block-center {
    text-align: center;
}
.inline-block-center div {
    display: inline-block;
    text-align: left;
}
```

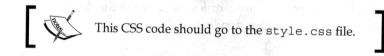

This CSS code should go to the `style.css` file.

Later on (**#8**), we loop through the list of services:

```php
<?php while ( $loop->have_posts() ) : $loop->the_post(); ?>
```

Next (**#9**), we add `$service_class`, which has the `perc` prefix (the percentage).

Then (**#10**), we define the services title and add a `service-title` class. We should also add the styling to `styles.css` for the `service-title` class:

```css
.service-title{
    color: #0480b5;
    font-size: 2.2rem;
    font-size: 22px;
    line-height: 22px;
    text-transform: uppercase;
    font-family: 'Open Sans', sans-serif;
    text-align: center;
}
```

This CSS code should go to the `style.css` file.

Next (**#11**), we add the `service-content` CSS class to the markup, and the code for that class should be the following:

```css
.service-content{
    margin: 20px;
}
```

Finally, (**#12**) we are displaying the content part with the_content() function.

As our services are nested in the `<section>` tag, here is more of CSS code that handles margins, padding, and a border:

```css
.services_section
  {
    margin: 20px 0px;
    padding: 10px;

}

section div {
    padding: 15px;
```

```
        margin: 5px;
        border-left-style: solid;
        border-left-width: 1px;
        display: table;
        border-color: #ececec;
    }

section div:first-child {
        border-left-width: 0;
    }
```

This CSS code should go to the `content.css` file's `desktop styles` media query:

```
        /*desktop styles*/
        @media only screen and (min-width:769px)
```

The `services` functionality is an extra functionality, which means that it is not a design/theme functionality and because of that, it should be put in a plugin as a separate feature. With this option, we give our end user a choice to use that functionality (or not) and at the same time, we follow the best WordPress practices (in this case, separating the content from design). Here is the link to a great article at *WP Tavern* that explains why we (the theme developers) are doing this: `http://wptavern.com/why-wordpress-theme-developers-are-moving-functionality-into-plugins`. There is a great library called the TGM Plugin Activation that we can use to require the recommended plugins, and it can be downloaded from `http://tgmpluginactivation.com/`. Covering this library is out of the scope of this book, but I strongly recommend that you use it.

Making our home page responsive

We have already started making our home page responsive by adding some code to the `content.css` desktop style media queries. Now, we should make some classes mobile phone friendly, and we will execute all these changes in the mobile phone styles media query in the `content.css` `@media` only screen max-width:480px.

At first, we don't really need a slider on the mobile phone size screen, so we should hide it:

```
    .metaslider{
        display: none;
    }
```

Then, we should take the display, flex, and the border from `section`:

```css
section {
        margin: 20px 0px;
        padding: 10px;
}

section div {
        padding: 15px;
        margin: 5px;
        border-left-style: none;
}

section div:first-child {
        border-left-width: 0;
}
```

Finally, we have to customize our percentage for services' CSS classes:

```css
.perc33{
        max-width: 100%;
        display: block;
}
.perc25{
        max-width: 100%;
        display: block;
}
.perc100{
        max-width: 100%;
        display: block;
}

.perc50{
        max-width: 100%;
        display: block;
}
```

With this code, each service will go into its own row.

Here is the final look on the mobile phone size screen:

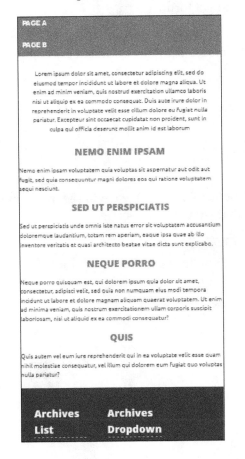

The Contact Us page

What would be the purpose of our business site if our customers can't contact us? This is why we are going to create a contact us page. Before we do this, we should install the Jetpack plugin as one of the options has a contact form plugin:

First (#1), we can see the **Contact Form** option, and then (#2), we should click on **Activate** to activate the contact form.

After we activate this option, we should create the **Contact Us** page, and in the editor, we will be able to choose the **Add Contact Form** option:

After clicking on **Add Contact Form** (#1), we will see the form builder where we will be able to choose fields that we want to use:

Add Contact Form

Here's what your form will look like

Name (required)

Email (required)

Comment (required)

This form doesn't have any kind of captcha option, as it is directly wired to the Akismet service, so it doesn't really need it.

Finally, after we accept all the options, the shortcode will be added to our form:

We will just have to publish the page, and that's it:

Summary

In this chapter, we have learned about static pages, slider, shortcodes, how to make our home page responsive, and how to create the contact us page.

By now, you should have a basic understanding of the development of a responsive theme in WordPress.

Now, the only thing left to do is to learn how to test our theme and how to properly submit it to WordPress.org by following the WordPress Codex.

Without further ado, let's move on to our final chapter.

10
Submitting Your Theme to WordPress.org

If you have been patient enough to stick with us until here, you should have a clear understanding of WordPress's responsive theme development and the steps involved in it. Your responsive WordPress theme looks beautiful and there is only one thing left to do before you introduce it to the world. Yeah, you guessed it correctly.

In this chapter, you will learn about fine-tuning your theme to follow the WordPress Codex in order to submit it to the WordPress.org repository.

There is still a lot of work left and without further ado, in this chapter, you will learn about:

- Polishing code before submission
- Applying the editor styles
- Validating the HTML and CSS code
- Validating the JavaScript and PHP code
- Adding the `readme.txt` file
- Adding the `screenshot.png` file
- Running a theme check plugin
- Submitting your theme to WordPress

Polishing code before submission

In order for our theme to be accepted, we have to make sure it meets the standards of WordPress.org, and in order to do that we have to test it and apply proper fixes. I have intentionally saved this for the last chapter as this should be the most important step before we submit the code to the WordPress.org repository. So let's do this together.

 Please check the look/behavior before and after applying each change as that is the best way to learn.

Let's take a look at the following steps:

1. On a `front-page.php` file please add this code:

    ```php
    <?php include_once(ABSPATH.'wp-admin/includes/plugin.php');
    ?>
    ```

    The preceeding code is added just before the code that checks whether the `nyto-services` plugin is installed:

    ```php
    <?php if ( is_plugin_active( 'nyto-services-
    cpt/nyto_services_cpt.php' ) ) {
    ```

    This code is adding the `plugin.php` library to the frontend pages as this library is used only in `wp-admin` backend. If we don't add this code to our home page, it will be broken.

2. When we check our theme on the cell phone, our main navigation is expanding too much on the sections where we have child elements. To fix this, delete the `position: relative;` property inside `.main-navigation ul ul` declaration which is located around line 623 in `styles.css`.

3. We want to have proper padding for our content when viewed on all devices. The best way to do this is to delete padding properties from class `.content-area` in all media queries (desktop, tablet, and cell phone) and just add this code:

    ```css
    .content-area {
        padding: 3rem;
    }
    ```

    The preceding code needs to be added to the neutral area (area before those queries) in the `content-sidebar.css` file. We are not adding that code to the `content.css` file as there we have the slider and code from the `services` plugin, and that content doesn't need any padding.

4. To make the header section with site branding look better, delete this code from `style.css`:

```
.logo-container {
    padding: 0 10px;
}
```

Then, add the following code to end of the `style.css` file:

```
.site-branding{
    padding: 1rem;
}
```

With this code, we are adding a padding of 1rem to our logo

5. In `style.css`, find the `.site-footer .widget` class and change it with this code:

```
.site-footer .widget {
    float: left;
    margin: 0 1rem 2rem 0rem;
    width: 30%;
}
```

This code makes sure that widget margins are proper (text or images are not going outside of their blocks)

6. If we are logged in in frontend preview, the `wp-admin` toolbar may be broken. Just delete `wp_deregister_style( 'open-sans' );` from `functions.php` in order to fix the broken `wp-admin` toolbar in frontend view.

7. We want to make the site's tagline to be of the same color:

In `style.css`, find the `.site-description` class and change the `color` property from #2B2B2B to #0480B5

In `content-sidebar.css`, find the `.site-description` class and delete the `color` property together with its value

In `content.css`, find the `.site-description` class and delete the `color` property together with its value

8. We now want to improve the look of services that are listed on our home page. Since we have borders and paddings there, we should update those classes in `content.css`:

```
.perc33{
        max-width: 31%;
    }
    .perc25{
        width: 23%;
```

```
    }
    .perc50{
        width: 47%;
    }
```

As we can see from the preceding code, we have just reduced the values in order to make the services fit in one row

Also, we should add this code to content.css in order to make sure our services are top-aligned:

```
.perc33, .perc25, .perc50,.perc100  {
        vertical-align: top;
    }
```

9. We also have to make sure that our blue color is the same in all places, so in `style.css`, change the background color from #579DB5 to #0480B5 around lines 542, 560, 581, 585.

    In `style.css`, on line 505, we should change `font-weight: 800;` to `font-weight: 500.`

    In `style.css`, on line 524, we should add `border-right: 1px solid #666;`.

    In `style.css`, on line 527, consider the following code:

```
.main-navigation a {
    font-size: 15px;
    font-size: 1.5rem;
    display: block;
    text-decoration: none;
    color: white;
    padding: 14px 10px;
}
```

Change the preceding code to:

```
.main-navigation a {
    color: #FFF;
    display: block;
    height: auto;
    margin: 0;
     padding: 14px 10px;
    text-decoration: none;
}
```

We have added `height:auto` here and have taken out the font sizes.

In `style.css`, on line 559, consider the following block of code:

```
.main-navigation li:hover > a {
    color: #FFF;
    background: #0480B5;
}
```

Change this to the following block of code:

```
.main-navigation li:hover > a {
    color: #FFF;
    background: #543018;
}
```

Here, we have changed the background color from blue to brown.

In `style.css`, on line 566, consider the following code:

```
.main-navigation ul ul a:hover {
    background: #0480B5;
}
```

Change this to the following block of code:

```
.main-navigation ul ul a:hover {
    background: #543018;
}
```

We have changed the background color here from blue to brown.

In `style.css`, on line 578, consider the following code:

```
.main-navigation .current_page_item > a,
.main-navigation .current-menu-item > a,
.main-navigation .current_page_item > a:hover,
.main-navigation .current-menu-item > a:hover {
    background: #0480B5;
}
```

Change this to the following block of code:

```
.main-navigation .current_page_item > a,
.main-navigation .current-menu-item > a,
.main-navigation .current_page_item > a:hover,
.main-navigation .current-menu-item > a:hover {
    background: #543018;
}
```

We have changed the background color here from blue to brown.

In `content-sidebar.css` and `content.css`, in `@media only screen and (min-width:769px)` and `@media only screen and (min-width:481px) and (max-width:768px)`, add the following code:

```
#menu-main-menu li {
    width: 130px;
    text-align: center;
}
```

Here we are making menu size fixed, `130px` on the desktop and tablet.

In `content-sidebar.css` and `content.css` in media query for phones, add this code:

```
@media only screen and (max-width:480px)
 #menu-main-menu li a{
    width: 100%;
}
```

We are making menu items to have a width of `100%` in mobile styles.

In `styles.css`, add this code to end of file:

```
.main-navigation
{
    font-size: 1.2rem;
    font-size: 12px;
}
```

Here we are making menu items to have the font size of `1.2rem`.

Finally, we have to make sure that all menu items are having the same right border. In order to do that, we have to add this fix to `global.js`:

```
jQuery("#menu-main-menu").addClass('clear');
    var containerheight = jQuery("#menu-main
menu").height();
    jQuery("#menu-main-
menu").children().css("height",containerheight);
```

10. In `functions.php`, find this code:

```
add_theme_support( 'custom-header', apply_filters( 'topcat_custom_
header_args', array(
        'default-image'          => '',
        'default-text-color'     => '000000',
        'width'                  => 150,
        'height'                 => 200,
        'flex-height'            => true,
        'wp-head-callback'       => 'topcat_header_style',
```

```
'admin-head-callback'     => 'topcat_admin_header_style',
'admin-preview-callback' => 'topcat_admin_header_image',
) ) );
```

Here, change the width and height as follows:

```
'width'                    => 220,
'height'                   => 100,
```

I think that the logo with bigger width and smaller height will fit better on our template and this is the fix.

Applying the editor styles

Before we submit our work to WordPress.org, we have to double-check our theme to make sure it's valid and meets all requirements of WordPress.org. As the _ **underscores** theme is a starter theme, it currently doesn't provide editor styles. Editor styles are the styles for the WordPress editor in **wpadmin** (the backend). The purpose of these styles is to match the look of pages or posts on frontend when the end user goes to the editor. For example, if we go to the `http://localhost/topcat/markup-html-tags-and-formatting/` post, we'll see the following screenshot:

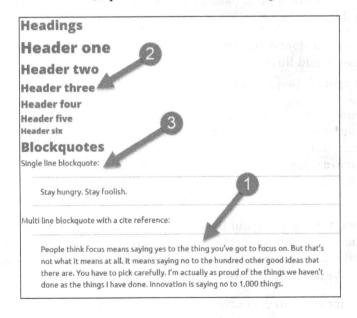

Then, if we open the same post in the editor in **wpadmin**, we get the following:

From the preceding screenshot, we can see that the font family is not the same (step 1), the font color is not the same (step 2), and the blockquote styling (custom HTML tag styling) is not applied (step 3). To fix this issue, we have to do the following two things:

11. Implement custom editor styles, `custom-editor-style.css`. In this file, we just have to add this code:

```
@import url( 'style.css' );
body {
    background: none repeat scroll 0 0 #FFF;
    font-family: "Open Sans",sans-serif;
    line-height: 14px;
    margin: 5px 10px;
    padding: 5px ;
}
```

Here, we are importing our theme's styles first, and then we are making sure that the background color is white in the editor (as from our theme's styles, the silver color would be the default one and we don't want that in the editor). We are making sure our font family is applied too.

12. Add editor styles in `functions php`:

```
function topcat_add_editor_styles()
{
    add_editor_style( array( 'custom-editor-style.css',
get_template_directory_uri() . '/css/open-sans.css' ) );
```

```
}
add_action( 'after_setup_theme', 'topcat_add_editor_styles' );
```

Here, we are adding our custom Google fonts and hooking our custom styles to the core. This is the result:

Headings

Header one

Header two

Header three

Header four

Header five

Header six

Blockquotes

Single line blockquote:

> *Stay hungry. Stay foolish.*

> *People think focus means saying yes to the thing you've got to focus on. But that's not w other good ideas that there are. You have to pick carefully. I'm actually as proud of the Innovation is saying no to 1.000 things.*

Validating the HTML and CSS code

In order for our theme to be accepted at WordPress.org, we have to validate our HTML and CSS code.

For this operation, I strongly recommend that you use two browsers [being logged in with one—for example, IE—and testing (logged out) with the other, for example, FF]. As you stay logged in in the FF, you might see some validation errors/warnings from the WordPress toolbar. As they are not our errors, they should be ignored.

For this purpose, I am using the Web Developer plugin for Firefox, which can be downloaded from this location: `https://addons.mozilla.org/en-US/firefox/addon/web-developer/`. When you install this plugin, you will get a Web Developer toolbar just under the URL (address) bar:

Mozilla Foundation (US) https://addons.**mozilla.org**/en-US/firefox/addon/web-developer/

Disable▾ Cookies▾ CSS▾ Forms▾ Images▾ Information▾ Miscellaneous▾ Outline▾ Resize▾ Tools▾ View Source▾ Options▾

The great thing about the Web Developer plugin is the validation options under the **Tools** section. If you want to validate the code without the plugin, you will have to go to the `www.w3.org` website manually. With the WD plugin, you just go to the **Tools** section, and you will be able to choose many options. My favorite timesavers are the **Validate Local CSS** and **Validate Local HTML** options. When we click on these options, our page will be validated against w3.org's validator, and we will see the following result:

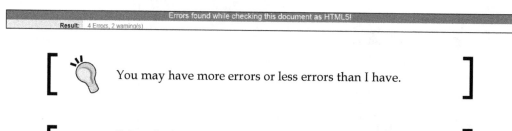

> You may have more errors or less errors than I have.

> Take a look at the results carefully. Some of the errors I've had were actually the errors of a Meta Slider plugin and we should not fix these as plugins are not part of our theme.

I would strongly recommend that you go trough as many posts as you can in order to validate HTML and CSS. If we are creating a custom page template, such as `front-page.php` in the previous chapter, we should also make sure that they are tested thoroughly. We should not have any errors or warnings there, although some posts use deprecated tags, like this one: `http://localhost/topcat/markup-html-tags-and-formatting/`. For this post, I've got a number of errors, for example, `The acronym element is obsolete. Use the abbr element instead.` These errors should be ignored, as these posts are just old examples.

I also strongly recommend that you subscribe to the theme review team mailing list, and if you have any questions, feel free to ask them there. The theme review team's page is available here: `https://make.wordpress.org/themes/`. I highly recommend that you follow the blog of the Automattic's theme division, which is available at `http://themeshaper.com/`.

Validating the JavaScript code

To validate and debug the JS code, I recommend that you use a **Console** tab in Firebug.

Firebug is an FF plugin that really helps with debugging HTML, CSS, and JS. It can be downloaded from `https://addons.mozilla.org/en-US/firefox/addon/firebug/`.

Chrome users should use Chrome Developer Tools, which are part of Chrome.

To access both of these tools, you can just press *F12* and they will show up on your page.

Now, just choose the **Console** tab in any of these tools and browse the test pages or posts. If there is a warning or an error, it will appear here.

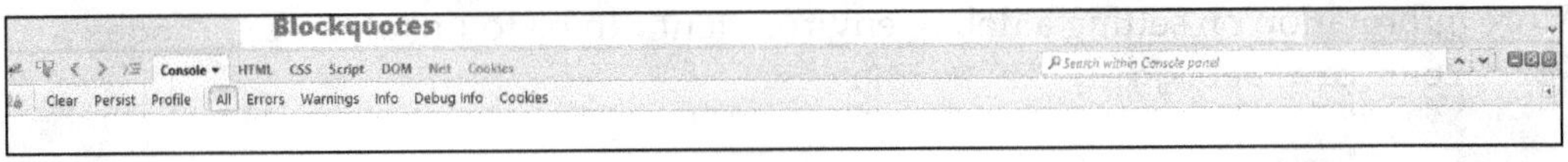

Validating the PHP code

The PHP code should be valid all the time, but sometimes, fixing errors and warnings just takes too much of our time. Displaying errors and warnings can sometimes be so distracting that we have to disable displaying them. If we do that, then we should fix these problems at least before we submit our code, in this case, the theme to the public repository.

Debugging the setup

In order to see the errors, we should add this code to the `wp-config.php` file that is located in the root folder of our WordPress installation:

```
define('WP_DEBUG', true);
// Enable Debug logging to the /wp-content/debug.log file
define('WP_DEBUG_LOG', true);

// Disable display of errors and warnings
define('WP_DEBUG_DISPLAY', true);
@ini_set('display_errors',1);

// Use dev versions of core JS and CSS files
(only needed if you are modifying these core files)
define('SCRIPT_DEBUG', false);
```

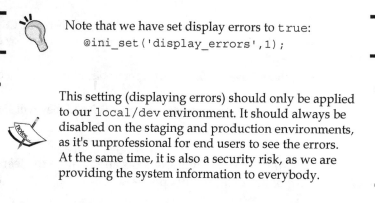

Note that we have set display errors to `true`:
`@ini_set('display_errors',1);`

This setting (displaying errors) should only be applied to our `local/dev` environment. It should always be disabled on the staging and production environments, as it's unprofessional for end users to see the errors. At the same time, it is also a security risk, as we are providing the system information to everybody.

More information on setting a debug environment can be found at `http://codex.wordpress.org/Debugging_in_WordPress`.

Multiple wp-config.php sets

As we want to test our code in as many different environments as we can, I recommend that you code and test in two environments: local (XAMPP on Windows) and dev server (Linux/Centos). Because of this, we have to have two different `wp-config.php` solutions as our credentials are different on different servers (and yours should be too). For this purpose, I am using a `wordpress-multi-env-config` setup that can be downloaded from `https://github.com/studio24/wordpress-multi-env-config`. Although this approach has a number of files, it's very easy to set up. In our setup, we should use:

- `wp-config.php`
- `wp-config.env.php`
- `wp-config.development.php`
- `wp-config.staging.php`

In `wp-config.php`, we should comment out:

```
// Define WordPress Site URLs if not already set in config files
/*
if (!defined('WP_SITEURL')) {
    define('WP_SITEURL', $protocol . rtrim($hostname, '/'));
}
if (!defined('WP_HOME')) {
    define('WP_HOME', $protocol . rtrim($hostname, '/'));
}
*/
```

In `wp-config.env.php`, we should set up our environments:

```
switch ($hostname) {
    case 'localhost':
        define('WP_ENV', 'development');
        break;

    case 'topcat.mywebsite.com':
        define('WP_ENV', 'staging');
        break;
/*
    case 'www.domain.com':
    default:
        define('WP_ENV', 'production');
*/
}
```

I strongly recommend that you set up at least a development and staging environment; if you have a similar setup, which means you have at least one local computer and server.

In `wp-config.development.php`, we should set database credentials:

```
define('DB_NAME', 'your_db_name');
/** MySQL database username */
define('DB_USER', 'your_db_user_name');
/** MySQL database password */
define('DB_PASSWORD', 'your_db_password);
/** MySQL hostname */
define('DB_HOST', 'localhost_or_your_servers_host_name');
```

We should also put here our debugging settings, which we just mentioned.

In `wp-config.staging.php`, we should have the database and debugging settings, and that's it.

If we have an error/warning or a notice, we should see something like this:

> **Notice**: Use of undefined constant topcat - assumed 'topcat' in **C:\Users\LPAC006013 \Dropbox\htdocs backup\topcat\wp-content\themes\topcat\inc\template-tags.php on line 129**

Let's see the code that was creating a problem:

```
echo edit_post_link( __( ' Edit ', 'topcat'), '|  <i
class="fa fa-pencil-square-o"></i>  <span class="edit">',
'</span>');
```

The issue here was that we didn't put the `topcat` value in single quotes.

Let's take a look at the comparison among notices, errors, and warnings.

The following data is found at `http://php.net/manual/en/errorfunc.constants.php`.

> *"Run-time notices. Indicate that the script encountered something that could indicate an error, but could also happen in the normal course of running a script."*

In our case, we didn't use the single quotes and our code didn't break the page, but it was pointed to us by the debugger that we should fix the code.

> *"Fatal run-time errors. These indicate errors that can not be recovered from, such as a memory allocation problem. Execution of the script is halted."*

This means that when we have errors in our code, it will break the page/script, and that should be fixed immediately.

> *"Run-time warnings (non-fatal errors). Execution of the script is not halted."*

This means that we are being warned of an issue but that issue is not breaking the code.

We should do our best to avoid having any of these (notices, errors, or warnings) in our production-ready code.

Adding the readme.txt file

Every theme that is submitted to the WordPress.org repository should have the `readme.txt` file. In that file, we should put the information regarding the theme's contributors/authors and tags that describe theme features.

The `readme.txt` file for our theme is available together with other files provided with this chapter and also on the GitHub page for our theme at `https://github.com/dejanmarkovic/topcat-final`.

Adding the screenshot.png file

The `screenshot.png` file is an important file as we can provide the screenshot or some other information regarding our theme there (in our case, we are providing the logo for our theme). The `screenshot.png` file should be of the size 880 x 600px or 387 x 290px. The `screenshot.png` file for our theme is available together with other files provided with this chapter and also on the GitHub page for our theme: `https://github.com/dejanmarkovic/topcat-final`.

More info regarding `screenshot.png` can be found at `https://codex.wordpress.org/Theme_Development#Screenshot`.

Running a theme check plugin

As we have validated all the code, we still have one more check to do, and that is to run a theme check plugin. Before we run it, we first have to enable it. To do that, we have to go again to **Developer plugin Tools | Developer** and click on **INACTIVE - Click to Activate**; the result is:

Theme Check	ACTIVE
Details	*A simple and easy way to test your theme for all the latest WordPress standards and practices. A great theme development tool!*

Then, we should run the theme check by going to **Appearance | Theme Check** and choosing our theme from the drop-down menu and clicking on the **Check it!** option:

After this, we will get a result like this:

As we can see from the preceding screenshot, we have to fix the things that are marked in red. All these errors/warnings are self-explanatory. The first two mention that we should take out Git references (directories and files) before we submit the code, as the WordPress.org repository is using subversion and also because we don't want to mix our own repository stuff with the public repository.

I also strongly recommend that you look into **RECOMMENDED** and **INFO**.

After we fix all the errors, we should go and submit our theme here: `https://wordpress.org/themes/upload/`.

I also strongly advise that you read the theme *Handbook* here: `https://make.wordpress.org/themes/handbook/review/`.

Summary

In this chapter, we learned about applying the editor styles; validating the HTML, CSS, JavaScript and a PHP code; running theme unit tests; and submitting your theme to WordPress.org. This concludes our book.

By now, you have learned how to develop a responsive theme in WordPress and how to submit the theme to WordPress.org, following the WordPress Codex.

You are now ready for your own WordPress theme adventure and that can be working for the agency by creating the themes, starting your own freelance business, or maybe starting your own WordPress theme development company. The choice is yours. Good luck in your future endeavors!

Index

Symbols

Thank you for buying
WordPress Responsive Theme Design

About Packt Publishing

Packt, pronounced 'packed', published its first book, *Mastering phpMyAdmin for Effective MySQL Management*, in April 2004, and subsequently continued to specialize in publishing highly focused books on specific technologies and solutions.

Our books and publications share the experiences of your fellow IT professionals in adapting and customizing today's systems, applications, and frameworks. Our solution-based books give you the knowledge and power to customize the software and technologies you're using to get the job done. Packt books are more specific and less general than the IT books you have seen in the past. Our unique business model allows us to bring you more focused information, giving you more of what you need to know, and less of what you don't.

Packt is a modern yet unique publishing company that focuses on producing quality, cutting-edge books for communities of developers, administrators, and newbies alike. For more information, please visit our website at www.packtpub.com.

About Packt Open Source

In 2010, Packt launched two new brands, Packt Open Source and Packt Enterprise, in order to continue its focus on specialization. This book is part of the Packt Open Source brand, home to books published on software built around open source licenses, and offering information to anybody from advanced developers to budding web designers. The Open Source brand also runs Packt's Open Source Royalty Scheme, by which Packt gives a royalty to each open source project about whose software a book is sold.

Writing for Packt

We welcome all inquiries from people who are interested in authoring. Book proposals should be sent to author@packtpub.com. If your book idea is still at an early stage and you would like to discuss it first before writing a formal book proposal, then please contact us; one of our commissioning editors will get in touch with you.

We're not just looking for published authors; if you have strong technical skills but no writing experience, our experienced editors can help you develop a writing career, or simply get some additional reward for your expertise.

WordPress Web Application Development

ISBN: 978-1-78328-075-9   Paperback: 376 pages

Develop powerful web applications quickly using cutting-edge WordPress web development techniques

1. Develop powerful web applications rapidly with WordPress.

2. Practical scenario-based approach with ready-to-test source code.

3. Learning how to plan complex web applications from scratch.

WordPress Complete

ISBN: 978-1-90481-189-3   Paperback: 304 pages

A comprehensive, step-by-step guide on how to set up, customize, and market your blog using WordPress

1. Clear practical coverage of all aspects of WordPress.

2. Concise, clear, and easy to follow, rich with examples.

3. In-depth coverage of installation, themes, syndication, and podcasting.

Please check **www.PacktPub.com** for information on our titles

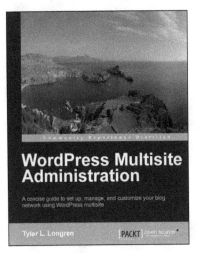

WordPress Multisite Administration

ISBN: 978-1-78328-247-0   Paperback: 106 pages

A concise guide to set up, manage, and customize your blog network using WordPress multisite

1. Learn how to configure a complete, functional, and attractive WordPress Multisite.

2. Customize your sites with WordPress themes and plugins.

3. Set up, maintain, and secure your blog network.

WordPress Plugin Development
Beginner's Guide

ISBN: 978-1-84719-359-9   Paperback: 296 pages

Build powerful, interactive plugins for your blog and to share online

1. Everything you need to create and distribute your own plugins following WordPress coding standards.

2. Walk through the development of six complete, feature-rich, real-world plugins that are being used by thousands of WP users.

3. Written by Vladimir Prelovac, WordPress expert and developer of WordPress plugins such as Smart YouTube and Plugin Central.

Please check **www.PacktPub.com** for information on our titles

CPSIA information can be obtained
at www.ICGtesting.com
Printed in the USA
FSHW020325280720
72261FS